TALK AND GROW RICH

TALK AND GROW RICH

How to create wealth without capital

RON HOLLAND

Thorsons
An Imprint of HarperCollins*Publishers*

Thorsons
An Imprint of HarperCollins*Publishers*
77–85 Fulham Palace Road,
Hammersmith, London W6 8JB

Published by Thorsons 1989

7   9   10   8   6

British Library Cataloguing in Publication Data

Holland, Ron
Talk & grow rich.
1. Salesmanship — Manuals
I. Title
658.8'5

ISBN 0 7225 1955 9

Printed in Great Britain by
Hartnolls Limited, Victoria Square, Bodmin, Cornwall PL31 1EG

CONTENTS

FOREWARNING

It is of paramount importance that you completely clear your mind of any preconceived ideas you may have of the ways and means people become rich and achieve success. You must empty your mind and become aware of the truths presented to you. The following story I include particularly for those who have heard it before — and not heeded the advice. Over a hundred years ago, Nan-in, the famous Zen Master, received a university professor who came to Japan to enquire about Zen. While Nan-in was quietly preparing tea, the professor began to elucidate at great length on all his own insights and philosophies. Nan-in had prepared the tea and began to pour the tea into the cup the professor was holding. When the cup became full, however, the Zen Master kept right on pouring and the tea overflowed everywhere. The shocked professor exclaimed, "But it is full, no more will go in." The Master replied, "Like this cup, you are full of your own opinions and speculations, how on earth can I show you Zen unless you first empty your own cup?" Will you grasp this opportunity to empty your own cup and fill it wisely with the proven formula for success that is expounded herein, or will you continue to search for the short cut to riches that has failed you so many times before?

FOREWORD

Writing the Foreword for a brand new international edition of my book is a very exciting prospect. It has given me the chance to say to myself, 'Now I have the opportunity to add or change things in the book, if I so desire, or maybe emphasize really valid points'.

The book has passed the test of time and I don't think there is anything I want to add or change. However, I have now had the advantage of a tremendous amount of feedback from many people who have bought and read the book. Having taken into account all this feedback from many readers over a long period of time, along with my own thoughts and meditations, I do think I have a message for you — it is the message of actually applying the principles of success.

Over the years I have received many letters from people in all sorts of situations and from all walks of life. Most people write in and thank me for the book, some include ways in which the book helped them, others want to know what else I have written and many request information about the Apprentice Millionaires' Club.

The other day I received a long letter from an elderly gentleman who was full of praise for the book. However, he went on to say that he'd read hundreds of books and he wondered when it was 'all going to happen' for him. I replied to this gentleman, and I'll tell you what I told him. Reading books on how to succeed is only the first step in the right direction. More important is that you actually apply the principles contained in these books to your situation. This takes time and effort and discipline.

I fell into the trap myself. A long time before my first success I used to lecture on the Principles of Success. My seminars revolved around one of the most important aspects of achieving success, which is the use of visualization. I remember going on and on with tremendous enthusiasm about visualizing the future as it is desired and seeing yourself as a success. I'm sure I convinced my audience, at least some of them. But I was not visualizing myself and, indeed, was having a job to make ends meet. It was only when I did take time out to visualize and meditate and really do the things with my mind that make the difference that things really started to happen for me.

I can tell you here and now it takes a great deal of courage to take the time to meditate and visualize when there are so many pressing things in one's life. I can also tell you, from first hand experience, that nothing great will ever happen to you until you gather the necessary courage and actually take time out to apply the principles of success and start doing the things with your mind that will actually make the difference.

One has to be constantly reminded actually to practice the principles of success. With this in mind, we set up the Apprentice Millionaires' Club. The club has a monthly newsletter with regular features, it is also a good way of getting to know other entrepreneurs all over the world. If you are interested in finding out more please write directly to Apprentice Millionaires' Club, 70 Tilehurst Road, London SW18 3ET.

In Australia write to Apprentice Millionaires' Club, P.O. Box 218, Westcourt, Cairns 4870, Queensland.

CHAPTER 1

THE PRINCIPLE OF POWER

"When you become quiet, it just dawns on you."

EDISON

It is highly probable that you are reading these lines while browsing in one of the world's multitudinous bookstores, contemplating whether or not to part with your hard-earned money in order to purchase a book. After a cursory glance at the chapter titles, what you read now will undoubtedly be the deciding factor in whether you make a purchase or place the book back on the shelf.

If I do have a claim to fame, it is generally recognized that I am a master of the Art of Persuasion. By using my art along with my knowledge of Dynamic Psychology it would be an extremely simple matter for me to contrive a convincing paragraph consisting of exactly what you want to hear; basically, how quickly and simply you can make your fortune and become an overnight success in whatever field you desire. Furthermore, I would convince you that we are both on the same wavelength and that I have a lot to say on a number of complex and controversial subjects that you will enjoy and appreciate. The proven method of inducing people to buy motivational books is to mix the basics up with a number of psychological words, a sprinkling of anecdotes, a liberal peppering of formulas, spread the mixture between the book covers with lashings of sincerity and persuasion and serve it up under the guise of a hypnotic "Get Rich Quick" title. Unfortunately, all too often, the readers of these books are the very same ones who complain quickly and bitterly that they have read reams of self-help material and still have not arrived at their goals.

This is the very bone of my contention. All too often self-help books are written with only one purpose in mind — to sell. The author himself may shy away from certain facts in fear of being labelled unorthodox, capitalistic, even Machiavellian. Editors may reduce the copy still further by editing out certain facts they consider will not make good copy, and finally the publisher may insist on reducing the script even further by taking out something he considers too controversial. In this writing of each page to sell, instead of writing each page as it really is, the reader is often deprived of many of the facts he desperately needs in order to succeed. If you are one of the many who have read a lot of self-help material, but have always been left short or stranded high and dry, you can now appreciate why!

To say that I am not interested in selling this book would be stupid — of course I want it to sell. But more than that, I am genuinely interested in producing a book that is foolproof in its instructions on how to grow rich. I want to produce a book that will fill the needs of every person who has failed in his or her endeavours; in particular, those people who have read a lot in order to attain their goals, but who still have not succeeded.

For far too long the intelligence of the reading public has been insulted by having important questions answered with questions, or what amounts to a play on words. Certainly hundreds of times, if not thousands, we have been told, "It is all in the mind," or, similarly, "Everything begins with the mind." No one ever says,

"If that is the case, why aren't all psychologists millionaires?" Time and again we are informed that the average human being uses only 15 per cent of his potential; never do we get a full explanation of why. Furthermore we are never shown how to realize the remaining 85 per cent.

Answering these questions formed the backbone of my research. Research, incidentally, that led me along many paths, up many blind alleys, and through much sifting of wheat from chaff. Ultimately, after many years of research my success philosophy is ready for the world. It will enable you to achieve your goals in the shortest possible time. It is a success philosophy to enable you to reach planes of abundance, have all the money you need to spend on your heart's desires and travel to all those exotic far off lands to see tranquil dawns and luminous dusks. It is your birthright to be able to obtain a pink Cadillac, a palatial Beverly Hills mansion complete with landscaped gardens, manicured lawns and a crystalline swimming pool and to be able to entertain frivolously, if that be your desire. Maybe you just want to get off the nine-to-five treadmill, or perhaps you have a very personal reason for wanting to be rich and famous. For all I know you are human like the rest of us and have funny quirks and traits. You may want riches to enable you to appear more attractive to the opposite sex. Perhaps you feel inferior and need wealth and recognition to show the world how great you are. It could be that you desire fame and fortune to compensate for some loss or misfortune. Whatever your reason, it is probably a good one!

Others will say some of life's finest things are not things. I agree, and there must be a way of achieving these intangible goals as well, whether they be peace of mind, love, health, happiness or power.

One staggering fact presented itself early on in my research and gave a granite-like foundation to the success philosophy presented here. By observing the fact that Henry Ford never had an industrialist to inspire him to become the apostle of mass production, Andrew Carnegie never knew any tycoons to coax him into becoming a billionaire, and Edison did not have a scientist show him how to become the world's most celebrated inventor, I saw that none of these people had a success philosophy to follow, a sponsor to motivate them or a yardstick by which to gauge their success. Nor did they have self-help books to assist them. However, all of them excelled in their individual fields of endeavour.

The Fords, Carnegies and Edisons of this world must have known some sort of secret or power to attain the phenomenal success each achieved in his particular vocation which, presumably, the layman had not heard of, nor had access to. I was particularly anxious to discover a common denominator, and whether that common denominator can still be applied to all human endeavour, even today. I found a common denominator of such extreme importance that it is outlined in detail in this very first chapter, entitled "The principle of power."

Imagine wanting to become a doctor, scientist, toolmaker, airplane pilot, cordon bleu chef, or master of any worthwhile profession, art, craft, skill or vocation. Imagine wanting to become any of these by simply reading a book. It would be an absurd notion. Nobody would expect to master any of the above without long and thorough training, practise and study. However, when we enter the world of fame and fortune, the majority of contenders expect to achieve their goals merely by reading shortcut plans to riches. The doctor, scientist or toolmaker understands initially that he will work out a long apprenticeship, gradually gathering up knowledge from people already trained in his profession. He will take exams, learn, study and practise until he becomes proficient enough to work with his own skills, and eventually without the supervision of his superiors and instructors. The books he uses in his studies are tools. As from this very moment you become an apprentice. An apprentice millionaire, a student of success. No less!

The first thing the apprentice millionaire must do is learn to be patient. Before the brain surgeon can put a scalpel to flesh, make that first incision, he has a lot to learn about the brain. Before the apprentice millionaire can *Talk and Grow Rich*, he too has a lot to learn about the mind and brain. Not only his own, but also his prospects'.

The starting point of my research was very simple. I wanted to find out if we really do use only 15 per cent of our potential. If that were the case, I wanted to know how to tap the remaining 85 per cent. I also wanted to know exactly what it is that is "all in the mind" and why "everything begins with the mind." I figured that if I knew the answers to these questions the acquisition of fame and fortune would be a relatively simple task. I took great pains to study much psychology and in doing so came across the brilliant works of the famous Swiss psychologist, Carl Jung. It was Jung's work that inspired me to do research along the particular lines that I chose. He, among others, noted that the people of the Eastern world are spiritually, mentally and physically more advanced than the people of the Western world.

We in the Western world are materialistic, but the people of the Eastern world know how to train their minds to achieve incredible feats. Through long and patient training of their subconscious minds, the mystics are able to perform unbelievable exploits. They train their minds to enable them to jab skewers in their backs and run needles through the palms of their hands without feeling pain or drawing blood. Although the Westerner has no use for the benefit of being able to perform such feats as these, we certainly do have a use for being able to control our minds so that we may prosper, and at the same time keep mentally and physically fit. All too often does the entrepreneur suffer from nervous exhaustion, stress, ulcers and lack of creative ideas and solutions to problems.

The obvious need (hence my research), was to harmoniously combine the knowledge of the East to complement the materialistic needs of the Westerner. One may call it turning Zen into Yen! The formula you need for all the wealth, success and achievement, and peace of mind, indeed for all the answers to all your problems, and I mean *all*, is S.S.S. — SILENCE, STILLNESS AND SOLITUDE. This is no invention of my own, and research into psychology and studies of world leaders, scientists, musicians, physicists, industrialists, inventors and other famous people proves this great power has been used, unwittingly or intentionally, since the beginning of time. All human success and achievement stems from this one power. It was used by Mozart, Einstein, Carnegie, Shakespeare, Emerson and Edison, to mention a few. This is the power used by the fakirs and mystics of the East and the fire walkers of the Fiji Islands. This power enables the mystics to sit naked in the snow for long periods of time, lash their bodies with whips, drink poison, and to jab nails and skewers into their cheeks and backs without feeling pain or drawing blood. It allows the fire walkers to walk barefooted across red-hot coals without feeling any pain. The secret lies in meditation, in silence, stillness and solitude. We shall call this S.S.S.

You must take time out. You must empty your mind. It is no good trying to think of your problems and sort them out consciously. You have been doing that for years, and where has it got you? However hard you try consciously, it will never work out the way you want. The secret of meditation is to hand over your problems to the subconscious mind, which is the master mind, the largest mind, the powerful mind, the creative mind. Think of an iceberg. You know that only one-ninth of the iceberg is visible, and the other eight-ninths of it are below the surface. That huge mass below the surface can be likened to the powerful creative subconscious mind. The small portion on top, the one ninth, is likened to the conscious mind.

Unfortunately, it is the conscious mind we tend to use. Wrongly so, for it is non-creative. The powerful subconscious mind, however, will only operate if given periods of S.S.S.

Alexander Graham Bell and Elmer Gates observed that the brain is both a receiving and a sending station for the vibration of thought. Imagine, then, sitting in a room with perhaps eight radios blaring away (for they, too, are receiving and sending stations) all of which are turned up to the same volume, but tuned into different frequencies. It would be impossible to decipher one from the other. For this same reason you can only hear your subconscious mind in S.S.S. Because, although you do not have eight radios blaring away, you do have a constant background of noise: telephones, radio, television; a motorcycle roars past, a child screams, a car revs up, a dog barks, an airplane flies over. The subconscious mind just cannot compete. Noise kills any hope of the subconscious mind communicating any enlightening ideas for the solving of problems, the making of money, the creating of happiness or the attainment of one's ambitions and goals. Noise kills genius!

When the world's greatest inventor, Edison, was asked how he solved problems, he replied, "When you become quiet, it just dawns on you." You are not required to think. You must take time out to meditate. I say again, not to think — but to empty your mind. "Thinking is the most unhealthy thing in the world," wrote Oscar Wilde, "and people die of it just as they die of any other disease."

The first thing you must do is find a place of your own where nobody can disturb you. You must have silence, you must be still and you must be on your own. Forget the gum and cigarettes for just half an hour every day. After you have been practicing meditation for a number of weeks, you will find you like it so much, that it will become one or two hours instead of half an hour. Sit either on the floor or the bed, cross-legged, with your back reasonably straight and gently clasp your hands in front of you. This is a very basic Yoga position. We can now assume you are in the desired position and have attained S.S.S. Now the secret is to empty your mind. This is more difficult than one would imagine. Try not to think of anything. Instead, concentrate on only one object. I choose to focus my attention on a glass prism, but any other object will do just as well. Just look at that object, think of nothing, breathe gently and relax. Try to think of absolutely nothing, for this is the secret of success.

To the layman this hardly seems a logical way of sorting out problems and generating "success ideas." It almost seems a waste of valuable time, with so much to do, so many pressures and problems. How then does it work? It is extremely simple. In the past you have let thoughts just fly through your mind, any thoughts at any time. Let us imagine that one hundred thoughts an hour go through your mind (in reality it is really thousands). If, in your meditation, you can reduce the number of thoughts going through your mind from one hundred an hour to only eighty thoughts an hour, that is an increase of 20 per cent efficiency. If you can reduce the number of thoughts to only fifty an hour, that is an increase of 50 per cent. The ultimate goal is to think of absolutely nothing. Then you can truthfully say that you have gained the power of concentrated thought by not thinking. It may seem paradoxical, but the mind is more creative when it is less active!

The great explorer, Rear Admiral Richard Byrd, understood what we are talking about. He was the

Commanding Officer of the United States Antarctic Service Expeditions. On the eve of his departure from the Antarctic, he broadcast: "It was on my lonely vigil during the long Polar night that I learned the power of silence. The values and problems of life sorted out when I began to listen. . ." Adopt the attitude of listening; not thinking. Silence is golden, silence is gold!

Because emptying your mind is so important, let us see if we can make an extremely difficult task more simple. Make sure the place you choose for your meditation is somewhere you will not be disturbed. The thought of being disturbed will constantly go through your mind if you know that someone can barge in on you. Personally, I prefer to go right up into the hills, miles away from anywhere and anyone. This is not always practical, but it is absolutely necessary that no one be able to disturb you. Solitude is the nurse of wisdom. I know that in some cities it is very difficult to achieve silence. Sometimes double glazing or storm windows reduce the noise level considerably. The local chemist will supply you with wax ear plugs and the do-it-yourself shop can usually supply earmuffs similar to those used by pneumatic drill operators.

I stress that noise kills genius. At first, you will find it difficult to sit still for half an hour, never mind a whole hour. You will probably get cramps and all sorts of uncomfortable feelings, but persevere, the rewards make it all worthwhile. Now for the actual emptying of your mind. The two things that will benefit your meditation greatly are a lighted candle and one of those digital clocks. To empty your mind for half an hour is not the easiest task in the world. However, until you become used to it, breaking down the half hour into thirty separate minutes is by far the easiest way of meditating. The idea is to say to yourself, "For the next minute I will think of nothing," stare blankly at the candle flame and think of nothing. Just wait for the next digit on the clock to come up. When it does, repeat the thought that for another whole minute you will think of nothing, just empty your mind and again wait for the next digit. You must bring to a halt the incessant chatter that goes on inside your skull, minute after minute, hour after hour, day after day, year in and year out. If you can turn down the noise in your mind, you can hear what else is going on. The noise machine in your brain box must be stopped!

It might help you to know I was a non-believer once, probably just as sceptical as you — dashing here, there and everywhere at breakneck pace, one side of the country to the other, visiting my shops and my businesses everywhere, radio blaring away all the time. At that time I hadn't heard the German proverb that asks, "What is the use of running when we are not on the right road?" One of my companies collapsed. On top of that, an employee embezzled a lot of money. Another company of mine was running at a loss. Thomas Fuller hit the nail on the head when he wrote, "He that is everywhere is nowhere." I was in such a state I could not think straight. I nearly burnt myself out. I thought I was going to self-destruct. I was numbed by it all, my brain nearly became addled. I found myself playing "beat the bailiff" and "bounce the cheque." I didn't know which way to turn — until I discovered the S.S.S. formula. I just started to sit still and empty my mind. Nothing at all happened for a number of weeks. Then things gradually started to take shape. I did not realize at the time I was unleashing a great power. Solutions to problems just came to me out of the blue. Illuminating ideas presented themselves and proved to be both practical and profitable, with unfathomable regularity. For once in my life things went right of their own accord; there was no help from me other than following through with the things my subconscious mind told me to do. I just sat still, quietly on my own, for an hour or two every day.

Shakespeare wrote, "There's nothing so becomes a man as modest stillness," and Dr. Paul Brunton said, "I have found that stillness is strength."

By meditating in S.S.S. you will begin to enjoy your own mind and until you can enjoy your own mind, you are doomed to fail. It was Plautus, the Roman author, who said, "If you have a contented mind you have enough to enjoy life with." It's a crying shame that many people do not have contented minds, but meditation in S.S.S. will cure all that. Regular meditation will put back the twinkle in your eye, the spring back into your step and the backbone into your spine. But all these are just side advantages, they are only the by-product of meditation. Regular meditation is also the solution to Public Enemy Number One: stress.

In the Himalayas, they say that the great secret of life is the achievement of action through non-action. Consider for a moment the sun. It is the star forming the centre of our system of planets. Everything in our solar system revolves around the sun. Every living thing on our planet is dependent on this one power, for without it all life would be non-existent in a few hours. Yet the sun is still, silent and in solitude. It does not rush here, there and everywhere, yet everything revolves around it. Consider the top executive of a large corporation. Does he run hither and thither, does he have people barging in and out of his office, does the telephone continually ring, is the radio blaring away in the background? No! He just sits there in S.S.S., yet everything revolves around him. Any telephone calls are first intercepted by any number of secretaries. People do not barge in on him because his aides and functionaries are there to see that they do not. His minions do the running for him. These analogies only serve to show that it is unnecessary to rush about with noise and in haste to achieve one's aims and ambitions, or to be in a position of power. Genius never hurries, unless one is an athlete or a racing driver. And the only place that happiness, money and fame come before silence, stillness and solitude is in the dictionary.

The Buddhists have a lovely little story relating to the principle of power. The gods were trying to think of a suitable hiding place for the principle of power so that mankind would not have the benefit of this great omnipotence. One god suggested hiding it on top of the highest mountain, but another god argued that sooner or later man would conquer even the highest mountain and find it. Another god suggested they hide it in the sea; he, too, was overruled by a god saying that man would conquer the depths and eventually find it. Yet another god put forward the idea of burying it deep underground, but like all the other suggestions this was overruled; as one god pointed out, man would excavate the earth. One wise old god, hearing the argument, put forward the motion that the principle of power should be hidden in man himself, for, as he pointed out, "Man would never think of looking there." The motion was carried.

Einstein obviously thought solitude was of great significance. His work was of immense importance, which included the paper on the theory of relativity and his famous equation $E = mc^2$ which opened the doors to the atomic age and, of course, led to the invention of the atomic bomb. The source of his power — which was solitude — is often overshadowed. In 1939 Einstein even wrote a letter outlining the advantages of solitude to the Queen Mother of Belgium. (It is also significant to mention that Einstein's lectures and papers raised millions of dollars for the war effort.)

Arthur Schopenhauer, the 19th century German philosopher, also thought solitude was of extreme importance and wrote, "Solitude has two advantages; firstly that one is with oneself; and secondly one is not together with others." And Ibsen got on the bandwagon with, "The strongest man in the world is he who stands alone."

All achievement, all earned riches have their beginning in an idea. But where do these ideas come from? You cannot just sit down and think of an invention, a best seller, a skateboard or whatever you consider a money-making idea. Ideas come to you when you are not thinking. I repeat, not thinking. This is the secret of meditation, to empty your mind. One of the greatest versatile geniuses the world has ever known was Leonardo da Vinci. He painted masterpieces, designed airplanes and built war machines. He had been only a man of talent, until he practiced emptying his mind. He used to stare blankly for hours on end at a pile of ashes. Suddenly his subconscious mind would give him astounding ideas. He was raised on to the plane of genius. By going *out* of our minds once a day we can come to our senses!

Do you feel like a matchstick on the top of a wave, being lifted up and crashed down with the tide? That is what happens when you listen to other people and to your conscious mind. If you were to listen to your subconscious mind, you would never make a mistake. You would go from strength to strength, making your own decisions, never faltering. Only the subconscious mind has this power. It requires no thinking, no effort. Just S.S.S. Perhaps the great poet Cary had this in mind when he wrote:

> Strive not to banish pain and doubt,
> In pleasure's noisy din.
> The peace thou seekest from without
> Is only found within.

William Wordsworth refers to "A happy stillness of mind." There is also in one of his poems the line "The world is too much with us." Take time out to meditate, to empty your mind. Be in this world, but not of it.

The relaxing and breathing is a very important part of meditation. The dried air of central heating is no good at all. The Tibetans sit cross-legged in the crisp, fresh, jasmine-scented air of the Himalayas, under a turquoise sky, amongst the deodars, neems and pines. That is the ideal. Get as near to the ideal as possible, even if it means going out into the country, or up a hill. Most people are too busy earning a living to make any real money, most people are frightened to take time out to meditate in S.S.S., and the average American works himself to death so that he can live. There is no need to be a workaholic, not when you mediate in S.S.S.

J. Paul Getty spent nearly six months of every year in the quiet English countryside at his Sutton Place residence. Howard Hughes spent the last fifteen years of his life in nearly total solitude; sometimes days would go by and he wouldn't even allow his Mormon aides near him. He bought tracts of land, hotels and gambling casinos in Las Vegas and nobody, other than a few aides, even saw him. Dr. Elmer Gates had a specially constructed soundproof room built where he could sit in S.S.S. and draw upon his creative subconscious mind. Some of the largest corporations in America paid him substantial fees for his ideas. He also created over two hundred useful patents.

Franklin D. Roosevelt spent long periods of time alone while recovering from a polio attack. Harry Truman spent time alone on a Missouri farm. John Bunyan spent years in jail in solitary confinement, where he wrote one of the world's greatest pieces of literature, *Pilgrim's Progress*.

You see, in the past your subconscious mind has told you to do many things. *Many* things. But you never heard, listened or obeyed. You thought you knew best, and where did it get you? You see, the power of the subconscious mind, powerful as it is, only impels. It does not compel. You can ignore your subconscious mind now, as you have done in the past. Unfortunately, you will not succeed in your ambitions and desires until you do learn to listen, to follow and to be guided by your subconscious. I cannot tell you more emphatically. Only you can decide your future. If you did only a hundredth of the research and study I have done into the human mind, you would see why. The conscious mind is non-creative, it is but an act. The subconscious mind (remember the iceberg?) — the greater portion, which is below the surface — is creative. It can build, plan, compute, assimilate and originate, it never makes a mistake. Never.

I take you back a few thousand years, and we find Aesop playing marbles on a cobbled street with some urchins. He is thoroughly enjoying himself and generally fooling around. Two elders come across and start to ridicule Aesop for playing marbles and silly games with mere boys. Aesop, as usual, explains that men of their wisdom never leave a bow with its strings in tension, but always take the strings off the bows, so that when they are needed they will be strong and powerful and ready for action. The human mind he explained, is the same. One must empty it and relax it, for a mind under continuous tension can be likened to the bow under continuous tension. The mind needs relaxation if it is to remain fit for concentrated thought. Now, I can already hear you saying "But I thought you said we don't have to do any thinking, you said the secret of success was not thinking." Let me explain further: you don't have to be thinking a thing, to be thinking of it. The best example is that of being lost for a word or a name, and when you had forgotten about it, when you were not thinking, out of the blue it came to you. Our subconscious mind still keeps on thinking although we do not realize it. It works away solving problems and creating success ideas twenty-four hours a day, and we don't even realize it. But when the subconscious mind hands over a solution to a problem or a "success idea" to your conscious mind you never hear it until you meditate in S.S.S. William James once wrote, "Compared with what we ought to be, we are only half awake, we are making use of only a small part of our mental resources.'' Now you know why.

Charlie Chaplin, one of the world's greatest actors, was renowned for taking time out in S.S.S. He used to sit on a deserted beach by some rocks for literally hours on end. He is not alone, for if you do some reading and research you will find that all great men, millionaires and tycoons do this, some of them without even realizing what they are doing. Winston Churchill, one of the world's greatest orators, used to spend hours on his own, and it was he who wrote, ''Solitary trees, if they grow at all, grow strong.''

Meditation in S.S.S. induces a state of calm, beneficial to the whole of the nervous system. That is why when you come back from a holiday your problems seem to have sorted themselves out. Because you forgot your problems when you were relaxing and enjoying yourself, your subconscious mind solved the problems for you. It came up with the answers you could never have thought of consciously.

Observe someone who you yourself personally consider to be great, wealthy or famous, and see whether they rush around in continual panic with furrowed brow and continuous frown. I can tell you here and now that they do not. This is because anyone who has reached a station in life where he may be termed successful has done so by following the directions of his subconscious mind, which shows you the easy, right and short-cut way to success. Let all your plans and behaviour have the same foundation.

Because meditation in S.S.S. is an extremely pleasant experience you must not get lulled into thinking that you can now sort our your problems consciously. This is wrong and must be avoided. It is admittedly an easy mistake to make — in all the quietness and being on your own and keeping still, there seems an ideal opportunity for sorting out life and its problems. Do not fall into this trap. By thinking consciously you will never receive the true answers to problems or generate real "success ideas." Without a doubt, you must empty your mind, think of nothing. What we are aiming for is something ultimately and infinitely more powerful than the conscious mind. By trying to sort out your problems consciously, even in S.S.S., you are defeating the whole object of the daily exercise.

Oh so many people want "peace of mind"; unfortunately, their lives are not geared to attaining it. Most cars are like jukeboxes on wheels. Everywhere you go you have a background of noise. You have heard the expression, "I can't hear myself think." Well, this is exactly what happens — with all that noise going on, you fail to hear your subconscious mind telling you the things to do to make you happy, to solve problems and start living. By having that radio blaring away and that constant background of noise, you are killing the goose that lays the golden egg, the subconscious mind.

Let us once again look at the saying they have in the Himalayas, "The great secret of life is the achievement of action through non-action." Well, it's like this: many millions of people, including yourself, have worked, strived and struggled, in fact carried out millions upon millions of actions, but where has that got them, or for that matter, you? Nowhere! You have not achieved your goals and aspirations. All your actions have been wrong actions. Through the practice of meditation we ensure that through non-action we make right actions!

It is important to clarify two points. The first is that, in S.S.S., we must attempt to reduce the continuous flow of thoughts that go through one's mind. There are many ways of referring to these thoughts: roof brain chatter, mind tape loop, incessant chatter in the skull, worries, or noise machine in the brain box — all refer to the thousands of unwanted thoughts that go through our minds hour after hour, day after day. The one term that includes all of these succinctly is "internal dialogue." Make sure you inscribe this phrase indelibly on your cranium, for it is going to crop up frequently throughout this book.

The second point I want to clarify concerns the "success ideas" that come to the quiet, receptive mind. These success ideas are sometimes known as hunches, inspirations or promptings of the subconscious mind, solutions that just come out of the blue, urges or gut feelings. The one term that includes all of these is Eureka! There is no limitation to the Eureka! experience; it can come as a fully blown success idea or just as a prompting. Eureka! means "I have found it." If you think a Eureka! only comes to a genius, this book will show you how to attain genius.

"I have discovered it" was the exclamation attributed to Archimedes upon discovering a method of determining the purity of gold. Archimedes also had a Eureka! experience when he got into the bathtub and, noticing the water level rise, discovered the way to measure the mass of irregularly shaped objects.

Eureka! is the motto of the state of California, which probably leads to the belief that all new ideas, worldwide, begin there. Certainly many trends, fads, crazes and ideas have come from California, but certainly not all.

Make more than a mental note of the word Eureka! because it crops up with the same frequency as "internal dialogue." For good reason, too: stop the internal dialogue in S.S.S. and you will hear the Eurekas!

If, when you began to read this, you said "I can't afford to take time out to meditate," you will by now surely realize that you can't afford not to!

ZOOM SECRETS!

1. Prepare a spare room for your own private meditation in S.S.S.
2. Buy wax ear plugs and a pair of earmuffs. Also use double glazing or storm windows to keep the noise level down. Noise kills genius.
3. Set aside at least 30 minutes every day — without exception — for your meditation.
4. To hear what your subconscious mind tells you, you must stop the noise inside your head as well as external noise. When you become quiet, "it just dawns on you."
5. You must follow through with what the subconscious mind tells you to do. As powerful as the subconscious mind is, it only impels. It does not compel.
6. The internal dialogue is the incessant chatter that goes on involuntarily within your mind. Eurekas! are success ideas that come from the subconscious mind. Stop the internal dialogue and you can hear the Eurekas!

CHAPTER 2

MIND POWER

"You can't lose with the stuff I use,
and the stuff I use is Mind Power."

REV. IKE

In the preceding chapter we just began to scratch the surface of the all-important non-thinking process. By now, it is apparent that it is of the essence to stop the internal dialogue to enable the Eurekas! from the subconscious mind to be heard. There are other types of non-thinking processes we must indulge in, but initially we must clear the path.

It is a frightening fact that of the four billion people who inhabit this planet, only a very small minority have their lives under control, are doing exactly what they want to be doing and as a result are happy and content. This is borne out by observing men and women everywhere. You can see the worried brow, the frown of discontent. You can feel the anxiety and tension; you can hear the constant bitching and moaning. Furthermore, all we have to do is look toward the doctors' offices, see them overflowing with patients suffering from psychosomatic illnesses, watch the number of prescriptions written out and the volumes of proprietary drugs and medicines sold over the counter. This tragic picture is glazed over with the millions of lost souls searching for highs in drugs, alcohol and depravity, hopefully to ease the burden of an already over-loaded mind.

The trouble with these people is that not only do they not try to stop the incessant chatter that goes on within their skulls, but, for the most part, do not even realize that the internal dialogue is with them all of the time. Of all the hundreds of thousands of thoughts that go through their minds every day, the thoughts that never dawn upon them are, "What is this incessant chatter within my skull? What is it for? How can I stop it?" Furthermore, they live from day to day following the conscious mind, which is strictly the "sleep when tired — eat when hungry" mind. Combine the foregoing with the desire for sex (which happens to be an extremely powerful driving force, and in many ways can be likened to that of the desire for food: just because you had a hearty and scrumptious meal on Monday doesn't mean you are not going to be hungry on Tuesday), and you have stumbled on the exact formula for how the majority of people run their lives.

Occasionally someone tries to crawl out of the rut. Only recently have we seen the ranks of meditators beginning to swell; but unfortunately the majority of them stop practising after a very short time. The practice of meditation originated in the East and it was primarily a device to enable one to attain spiritual fulfillment. When the materialistic Westerner adopts the practice it hardly ever comes up to his expectations, usually because he is lacking direction (assuming, of course, he is really meditating both properly and regularly). The Westerner interested in material gains must be shown how to utilize the 85 per cent of the potential mind power that has until now been untapped.

By tapping the 85 per cent of unused potential, we soon realize we are using parts of the mind that have previously been dormant, and one realizes that there are many states, levels or zones of consciousness. We realize that it is a stupendous part of the mind we haven't used. It is generally recognized that up to 45 states of consciousness can be induced and attained by drugs and artificial stimulants, but that up to 165 states can be achieved by the Eastern mystics solely by meditation and correct preparation. (There is no definite agreement about the names and numbers of states of consciousness.)

I wouldn't take William Hazlitt to task just because he wrote ''The definition of genius is that it acts unconsciously; and those who have produced immortal works have done so without knowing how or why,'' but what I will say is that although genius does act unconsciously (or rather subconsciously) we definitely do know why and, beyond a shadow of a doubt, we do know how.

Basically, for our intents and purposes — that of making money and achieving success — we must deal with the mind on three levels. The subconscious mind, which is the largest mind, is analytical, since it creates, computes, plots, plans and never makes a mistake. It is the mind we seldom use. Because of all the noise within our minds and around us we never hear it. Next, we have the unconscious mind, which has stored in it all the knowledge of everything we have done and everything we have experienced from the moment of birth. Any inhibitions or fears which we happen to have originate deep down in this mind and though we don't realize it, because it is so deep down, it affects our daily lives, albeit unconsciously. Then we have the conscious mind, the mind you are using now to comprehend and assess what you are reading. You also use it for writing, talking, learning and everyday observation. It is but an act. It is strictly the ''eat when hungry — sleep when tired'' mind.

Let us look individually at each of the three minds to see exactly how we can use them in a way that will be tapping the huge reservoir of potential so few of us use but that so many of us talk about.

THE SUBCONSCIOUS MIND

When computer programmers say, "GIGO", they simply mean that if you program the computer with garbage, all you will get out of the computer is garbage, hence, "GIGO" — garbage in, garbage out. In many ways, ways the subconscious mind can be likened to a computer — a million dollar computer, no less. The subconscious mind knows and recognizes your predominant desire, picks up facts, assimilates them and organizes them into an infallible plan to enable you to attain whatever the predominant desire happens to be. When it has completed its computerized labour it brings the idea into the conscious mind in the form of a Eureka!

Should you be feeding into your subconscious mind feelings of negation, fear, poverty, disease and destitution, the subconscious mind will loyally carry out plans for the attainment of such. On the other hand, should you feed in visions of success, wealth, fame and fortune, the subconscious mind will create the necessary plans for the attainment of same. It gives you exactly what you ask for. This is exactly what Emerson had in mind when he wrote, "Be careful what you set your heart on, for it surely will be yours."

Programming the mind to enable us to attain our worldly desires is done through the practice of visualization. This is the practice of seeing your desires in your mind's eye every night before retiring and every morning when you rise. If you desire a pink Cadillac, visualize it clearly in your mind's eye. Feel the cold air on your face from the air conditioning, feel the power as you accelerate. See the tinted glass and the honeycombed magnesium wheels. Switch on the stereo, get in and out of the car, feel it, believe you own it. The language of the subconscious mind is the repetition of mental images.

Napoleon Bonaparte was an avid practitioner. He used to see himself as the General of Armies and the

Master of France. He used to go on manoeuvres and practise strategy. He practised soldiering, all in his mind's eye, before he ever saw a battlefield.

The subconscious mind always provides plans for the attainment of your predominant desire or desires, it never fails. If it is a million dollars you desire, see the money clearly in your mind's eye. See the bank statement with your name on it, run your fingers through the money, believe it is yours. Do this every night and every morning. Do not think of how you will accomplish such a feat, that is not your business. That is the job of the subconscious mind, it needs no help from you, no thinking about how you will attain your desires. However, the subconscious mind does require the repetition of mental images and periods of S.S.S.

The renowned psychologist, William Moulton Marston, used to get people to rehearse in their mind's eye. If someone came to him wanting advice on his or her career he used to get them to visualize themselves in the "position" they required. "Rehearse the future as it is desired," he told them. It is imperative that you see your desires clearly in your mind's eye, be they material or intangible goals. Reading your desires, parrot fashion, from a list will bring no results whatsoever, and it is essential that you visualize every night and every morning. It is of no use at all to practice only when you feel like it. It is of the essence that you believe your goals have already materialized and it is similarly important that you do not think of how you will achieve such ambitions. As Paracelsus, the great physician, said, "Those who make room for impressions, receive them."

If you want to become an actor, film star, or politician, see yourself in your mind's eye already doing these things. Visualize whatever it is you desire to be or long to possess. Supercharge the atmosphere with these thoughts, emotions and images and the belief that you are, you do, you own.

When the great pianist Arthur Schnabel was asked how anybody could be such a brilliant pianist with so little practice, he replied, "I practise in my head." In a similar vein, an Olympic gold medalist was lounging in his hammock when his coach appeared. The athlete, who was a pole vault champion, asked the coach to move the bar up to the next peg. The coach was puzzled because he knew the athlete had not jumped the earlier setting. When asked, this athlete, too, replied that he was practicing in his head.

Through the practice of visualization the mind cannot fail to come up with illuminating plans for you to achieve, attain and build. How does it do this? Ralph Waldo Emerson knew the answer: "Each mind has its own method." The subconscious mind works on your predominant desire, it will go about its business picking up facts for its computer although you will be totally unaware of it doing so. I want to give you a simple illustration of how the subconscious mind works; you see, the more you can understand how it works the easier it is for you to see exactly what you are trying to achieve.

The first example is about a young woman who wanted a piano. She desperately wanted a piano, and although she could not afford one she believed that before long she would own one. It was her predominant desire. She believed in the thought and cherished it. Every day when she did the dusting she would dust the imaginary piano. She knew within her heart of hearts that before long she should possess one of her very own. While quietly meditating one day, she had a certain feeling come over her. She did not know why, but she did know it was her subconscious prompting her to go to the local village green. When the young woman arrived, there was to her amazement a fair in full swing; flashing lights, organ music, cotton candy, taffy apples and amusements. What caught her eye next was something truly amazing — a piano smashing stall where you could pay a few pennies to try your hand at smashing a piano with a large hammer. The young woman hurried onto the stand, and, with a smile in her voice, said to the boy running the stall, "What a pity to break up such lovely pianos, when here I am longing for one but can't afford it." Equally pleasantly the young boy replied, "Lady, if you want a piano just say the word; I'll even have it delivered, with my compliments." That is how the young lady came to be in possession of her piano. Now on the psychological side, we should examine how the subconscious mind worked this little trick. Without the young lady realizing it, the subconscious mind probably saw an advertisement for the fair in the newspaper. It could have been a poster on a wall somewhere, or it could have remembered that at this time every year there was a fair on the village green and that one of the stalls was piano smashing.

One point I make quite clear is that visualization and meditation are based on psychological laws, not magic! Providing you meditate and practice visualization, the subconscious mind is bound by psychological law to provide a plan for the attainment of your desires.

The next illustration is equally simple and concerns a young engineering enthusiast who rebuilds vintage motorcycles as a hobby. He not only rebuilds them but he makes absolutely sure they are completely authentic, original and *concours d'elegance*. However, a particular motorcycle, an "Indian," I think he called it, was short of one item, the carburettor. All he needed was a carburettor and his lovely project would be finished. He never gave up hope; he believed that somehow he would get hold of the part. He saw the motorcycle in his mind's eye, it was running like a sewing machine, it had a carburettor on it. He believed with all his heart that somehow a carburettor would come into his possession. One day, while not thinking of anything in particular, he had a notion that he must go down to the local scrap yard. On his arrival and to his disappointment he found the scrap yard closed for the day. As he was looking curiously through a crack in the fence, the voice of an old man startled him. "Can I help you, son?" said the old timer. The boy jumped with shock and then told the old man the story of the missing carburettor. For some reason or other the old timer was particularly amused. "Come with me, boy," he beckoned. The youth followed him into an old derelict shed where the old man rummaged around and eventually found the exact carburettor the boy was looking for. Now when I say exact, I mean exact, for it was the actual carburettor that was missing from the young man's "Indian." It transpired that a few years previously the old timer had sold the motor-cycle but had misplaced the carburettor, and the new owner had lost interest in the project and sold the motorcycle to the young man in our story.

Back to the scientific, or if you like, the psychological explanation. The subconscious mind may have remembered the old timer, who lived next to the scrap yard, originally advertising the "Indian" for sale. We can't be sure really, but this is what the sub-conscious mind does, if you give it half a chance. It serves little or no purpose to expand the facts or the example. This is the point I am trying to make: the subconscious mind is creative. To create you must have something to build with. It will automatically pick up facts and information without you knowing or thinking. It will create plans for you that you would never have thought of consciously in a million years.

Do not misunderstand what is being said. When you visualize your desire, you will be shown how to attain that desire or its equivalent. The boy who got the carburettor might not necessarily have obtained the original item, but he would have obtained its equiva-lent, which would have been quite sufficient and acceptable. This example was used particularly to show you that the subconscious mind works with the material at hand.

If you eat, drink, talk and visualize poverty, your subconscious mind will build and create plans for you on this level. The language of the subconscious mind is repetition of mental images. Whatever it is that you see for yourself in the mind's eye, the subconscious mind will create a plan for its attainment. By feeding our subconscious mind mental images of the things we desire, we give it the material it needs to use as a basis for its creativity.

The foregoing examples are true accounts of how the subconscious mind works. There is nothing extraordinary about this, nothing spooky about the way it works. In fact anyone who visualizes a predominant desire and gets periods of S.S.S. will be shown how to attain through the use of his or her subconscious mind. The powers of your subconscious mind are limitless. Although the foregoing is only an introduction to the subconscious mind, you are already beginning to see the potential and how it works while not thinking.

Another aspect of the subconscious mind is that of problem solving. One of the best things you can do is to accept the fact that everybody has problems. A famous sage once said, "You can have anything you like in this life, I repeat anything, providing it is not a life free of problems." The secret of success is to accept that we all have problems but to acknowledge the fact that people who remain happy and unperturbed by them know how to sort them out.

How is it that some people have the knack or the ability to sort out problems with relative ease and with relatively less pain than others? The answer lies in the subconscious mind. The answer also lies in not thinking. The subconscious mind will solve all problems for you with solutions so accurate and revealing you will wonder how you lived without using it. The answer is simple — you didn't live, you merely existed. With the aid of the subconscious mind you can now live as you have never lived before. Solutions and ideas come out of the blue. Problems will vanish as if by magic. The only catch is you must use the subconscious mind in your problem solving efforts. The way to use the subconscious mind is simple.

Write the problem down, no matter what it is. Define it, i.e., whether it is personal, mental, emotional or financial. Get the problem down on paper as accurrately as you can. You then write down all the possible solutions, no matter how utterly mad or seemingly impossible they may look. Write down as many possible solutions as you can to each specific problem. Now examine each possible solution and as you examine the possibility of each solution, one of two things will happen. The first possibility is that you will find a solution to your problem. In that case, fine. You need not enlist the subconscious mind to your aid. If, however, you still have no solution to your problem, all you do is hand it over to the subconscious mind. You do this by saying, not aloud but within yourself, ''Subconscious mind, I hereby hand over the problem of _____ for you to solve.'' Give the subconscious mind a specific time limit in which to solve your problem. Make this time limit as long as possible, a week or a month if the problem is a big one. The subconscious mind will solve the problem in a matter of hours if it has to, but generally speaking the longer you give it the better. The secret of the success comes in not thinking — once you have handed it over to the subconscious mind, do not think about it. Forget it! The subconscious mind is more than capable of solving problems on its own, it needs no meddling from you. Within the time limit, the subconscious mind will come up with a solution to your problem. It will feel right, you will know it is right when it comes. Put the solution into operation immediately. The subconscious mind does not like solving problems unless the solutions it presents are used. If you don't use the solution supplied by the subconscious mind it will be some time before it will function properly again. So, to recap, here is what you do:

1. Write down the problem and define it.
2. Write down all possible solutions, even seemingly mad or impossible ones.
3. As you go through the list, eliminate those which you decide will not solve your problem.
4. Hand the problem over to the subconscious mind with a specific time limit (as long as is possible).
5. *Do not think about it* once you have handed it over to the subconscious mind.
6. When the solution comes, use it!

Many times you have used the subconscious mind without realizing it. The obvious example brings us back to the word or name that was on the tip of your tongue but which you could not remember. However, sometime later, while not thinking, the answer came to you out of the blue.

We have just discussed two very important aspects of the subconscious mind. In the subsequent chapters we will not only go deeper into visualizing but also into many aspects of the subconscious mind. It is important that you never lose sight of the fact that the subconscious mind is in charge and its size accounts for eight ninths of the mind.

THE UNCONSCIOUS MIND

Deep down in the unconscious mind lie all the reasons behind any inhibitions, hang-ups or fears that one may have. The secret of success is to draw these inhibitions, or rather the cause of the inhibitions, to the surface, into the conscious mind. Today this is a world-wide billion-dollar industry. We call it psychoanalysis, and it often enlists the aid of drugs or hypnosis. But what psychologists have been practising for a few decades has already been practised for thousands of years. In the golden age of Greece, at the time of the great philosophers, the words "Gnothi Seauton" were inscribed in large letters over the entrance to the Athenian Temple. Translated this means "Know Thyself", which was considered then to be absolutely essential to all knowledge by the wise men of the time. In Tibet and India, the mystics would not contemplate swallowing poison or passing skewers through their cheeks without self-knowledge.

Psychologists have found the strongest possible evidence that inhibitions are formed in early childhood beginning with "toilet training". Should a child be chastised instead of gently encouraged to use toilet facilities properly, trouble begins. As the child grows older, if he is not encouraged in small things, he will never entertain ideas of anything on a larger scale. The young boy in the hobby shop who is encouraged by his father to chisel, hammer and saw will become a self-reliant adult, whereas the youngster who is reprimanded and told he is useless and to get out of the way will become a burden on society. He will undoubtedly end up with what we call today an inadequate self-image (years ago we called it an inferiority complex).

In Tibet, where self-knowledge is a necessity for spiritual attainment, a Yogi in his meditation will start where he is and retrace in his mind every action he performed that day. Then he will retrace all the actions made the previous day, going further back throughout his life. It has been said that after many years' practice the Yogis can remember right back to the moment of birth.

In essence we do the same thing by asking questions and gathering information about our childhood. Friends, relatives, and old photographs all build a picture of our upbringing, so that we may find out if we were repressed during childhood. Obviously we only need do this if there are hang-ups and inhibitions. By doing unnecessary analysis you will be creating problems where none exist.

It was Jung who coined the phrase, "All self-analysis without confession is futile." You must write down all your fears and inhibitions; the paper will be for your eyes only, and after analysis it can be destroyed. The function of the exercise is to list all your fears and inhibitions and then analyse childhood experiences to see why the fears and inhibitions exist. Only then will you *Know thyself*. In the words of Harry Emerson Fosdick, "To get our fear out in the open and frankly face it is of primary importance." Only when you have dispelled fear from your system will you be a success. No one knew this better than Carlyle, and he put it very succinctly: "The first duty of man is that of subduing fear; he must get rid of fear; he cannot act at all till then, his acts are slavish, not true."

The second part of the exercise is to lay the ghost of fear to rest. We do this by bringing the fear or inhibition into the forefront of the conscious mind and then we "laugh it out of court" by gradually doing the thing we fear. By laughing at it we overcome our hang-ups, inhibitions and fears.

When an aeroplane test pilot crashes, the first thing he does is to get back in an aeroplane as soon as he can — if he didn't do this he would soon lose his nerve. Likewise the racing car driver; if he has an accident he must immediately get back in a car and drive as fast as he can. If you are afraid of talking to people or going out on your own, these are the things you must do. Not all at once, but gradually, step by step. By far the most powerful tool you have now is the subconscious mind. If you listen to it you will be warned of any impending dangers. Anyone who takes time out in

S.S.S. need have no fear whatsoever for he or she will be shown a clear and safe path.

THE CONSCIOUS MIND

Let us examine the conscious mind and see how we can most benefit from it through the practice of not thinking. You are using the conscious mind now, this very minute, to comprehend what you are reading. You also use it for learning, writing and watching television. How can we progress quicker? How can we make full use of the conscious mind using the non-thinking processes? The answer is simple. Enthusiasm! Let me give you a graphic example of what I mean.

Imagine you are madly keen on auto racing. Without thinking you gather a pile of good usable knowledge: the types of cars, brake horsepower figures, the types of fuel injection used, compression ratios, drivers' names, mechanics' names, last five years' winners, lap times, speeds and so on and so forth. You pick up the knowledge as you go along, through sheer enthusiasm. Consider now a different subject, one that you are not madly keen about. In fact you hate it. For argument's sake let us say it is history. You have to try really hard to remember dates, names, facts and happenings. Sometimes it doesn't matter how hard you think, you still cannot remember. You are not enthusiastic. The information you pick up at auto racing is probably far more technical and complicated than many historical facts but, without enthusiasm, it becomes impossible to learn, store, remember and recall such knowledge. That great essayist, Emerson, observed this fact and it prompted him to write, "Nothing great was ever achieved without enthusiasm."

You probably haven't felt enthusiastic for years. You know what I mean. With real enthusiasm, nothing is too much trouble, you feel as though you could dance all night, sing in the rain, the tiredness falls away. Life is a labour of love, and that is how it should be. If you are not happy now, wildly enthusiastic about your job, your friends, life, everything, what is it all for? You're a long time dead! I know it is all very well for me to talk and you would love to be enthusiastic again, if only you knew where to begin. Well, by cultivating your mind in S.S.S. you will be shown health, happiness, love, fame and fortune. At the moment, you are doing too many of the wrong things and certainly not enough of the right things. You will never attain peace of mind until you become still, you will never feel enthusiastic until you begin to do the things you feel you ought to be doing. Your life is not under control, you are not having the vacations you want, you are not enjoying the hobbies that you want to spend time at. You are in too much of a hurry all the time. I know, you have got this bill to pay, that problem to sort out, this relationship to end, hopefully another one to begin, that emotion to resolve, this depression to lift. Of course I know all of your problems. You don't think I have devoted a lifetime to studying psychology for nothing. The only reason I have left out some of the problems that beset you is because we would need a book the size of a telephone directory to get them all in.

The problem or question of enthusiasm cannot be answered in just a few sentences. It has so many components, which fall into so many categories, that the answers about enthusiasm have been spread throughout the chapters of this book. A few of the components that will bring back long lost enthusiasm are S.S.S., knowing what you want out of life, actually achieving those things and doing your own thing. By the time you have finished this book you will have all the enthusiasm you need. But for the time being I want you to remember that enthusiasm is necessary for the achievement of any goal.

The centre of the conscious mind is the ego. The ego works without thinking and if we realize that all minds operate like this, not just our own, we can use it to great benefit. If you take a shower, dress right up, put on some gold and diamond rings and some expensive jewellery, you feel refreshed, you feel like a different person. Your ego is boosted even if you only borrowed the regalia. When people meet you dressed this way they will treat you like a different person. They will treat you with respect. On the contrary, if you dress like a tramp, unshaven, exuding body odour, people will treat you like a tramp. For all they know you could be a millionaire or a genius, but, without thinking, their egos accept the idea that you are a tramp, or a down and out — and this applies not only to their egos but to your own as well. The ego of the conscious mind accepts whatever is put in front of it without asking questions and without thinking. We can use this psychological knowledge to our advantage. If you want to be a great person act as though you were a great person. If you want to be a star salesman act as though you are a star salesman. Whatever you want to be *act as if* and it will be. Theodore Roosevelt once said, "There were all kinds of things I was afraid of at first but by *acting as if* I was not afraid, I gradually ceased to be afraid. Most men can have the same experience if they choose." (My italics.) Without a question of a doubt you must choose to "act as if," if you are to attain. You can "act as if" in any circumstances you desire.

Over a hundred years ago Goethe wrote: "Whatever you can do, or dream you can do, begin it. Boldness has Genius, Power and Magic in it." Act as if you are confident — and nothing will stop you from attaining.

THE SIXTH SENSE

Some years ago a little schoolboy was asked by his teacher to write an essay on "The funniest thing he had ever seen." He wrote just eleven words: "The

funniest thing I ever saw was too funny for words!"
Well, let me tell you, that is exactly how I feel — lost
for words, because the sixth sense almost defies description.

Let me tell you first what it isn't. It must not be
confused with the subconscious mind; and unlike the
other parts of the mind, you cannot order the sixth
sense to work for you at will. The three minds we have
already discussed take and compute knowledge gained
by the five senses. Through the sense of hearing we
listen to the spoken word and music as well as all the
noises of the world. Through the sense of sight we are
able to appreciate nature and colours; you can also perceive through the eyes. Through the sense of smell we
can detect smoke, dinner and perfume. Our sense of
touch tells us what is smooth, rough, hot or cold. And
our sense of taste allows us to enjoy lobster thermidor
and champagne. All knowledge gained by these senses
allows the three parts of the mind to operate in the
ways we have discussed.

However, the sixth sense does not operate through
these. It requires no previously gathered knowledge, it
operates on indirect spiritual and metaphysical percep-
tion. One might say that the subconscious mind is a
million dollar computer but the sixth sense is your
billion dollar computer *and* life saver combined.

The sixth sense comes to your aid when you are
least expecting it and comes into operation without
your thinking about it. So magnificent and rapid are
the manoeuvres it computes for us that it short cuts the
whole nervous system and the whole thinking system.

Any emergency which arouses the emotions and
causes the heart to beat more quickly can bring the
sixth sense into operation. The sixth sense will come
to your aid whether you are driving a car, running
your business, or whatever you are doing when you
happen to get into an emergency situation.

The easiest way to explain the sixth sense is to mention the example of a man who was driving his car extremely fast, when suddenly a car pulled out in front of him and smashed a car coming in the opposite direction, leaving cars and debris right in his path. When he was with his associates later in the day he described his lucky escape: "I didn't have time to think, I just swung the wheel round, braked hard, then accelerated and I missed both the other cars. A sixth sense, I suppose." You hear this kind of story every day in one form or another. The sixth sense operates in "on the spot" circumstances, it acts instantaneously.

The ability to use this omnipotence comes slowly; you must develop it. Within this statement lies the answer to the reason why some people die in automobile accidents and others allow the sixth sense to mysteriously guide them through danger. It would appear that the sixth sense will not work instantaneously for those who "sit on the fence" and let everyone else do the work, take the blame or shoulder responsibility. It would appear that it comes to your aid when you risk everything; in fact, put your very life on the line.

So how do we cultivate this omnipotence? Obviously, in S.S.S., but that is only a start. Another thing we can do is to live more dangerously. Now I certainly don't mean racing down the High Street at 130 miles an hour in a Porsche, but I certainly do mean getting a bit more involved in life and taking a few more risks. It is a well-known psychological fact that well-balanced people have danger, fear, excitement, risks and thrills as part of their diet. Whereas mentally unstable people do nothing, live humdrum existences and mollycoddle themselves. Here lie the sad, bad and the mad.

It is strictly up to the individual, but all you need is a bit of imagination. Here are a few of the things I have done personally to help me develop my sixth sense in order to achieve my personal and financial goals. I bought a motorcycle. There is nothing like having the full blast of fresh air in your face — that motorcycle opened up a whole new life, a tingle for adventure. Of course I have always had sports cars and I enjoy driving fast. I went mountaineering, not to the top, but high enough to make my heart beat faster. I bought a small boat — I didn't use it a lot, but when I did, it was great fun. Now I am not saying I spent a fortune on these gizmos to enhance my life and to enable me to develop my sixth sense, because I didn't, and you need not either. But at any cost you must get a bit of danger and a slice of fear, a portion of excitement into your life. Cultivate the sixth sense like this and you will think a miracle has happened when it comes to your aid without even split seconds to spare. You never know when the sixth sense may even save your life, never mind get you out of a financial fix or come to your aid when the chips are down; it has done so for me on more than one occasion.

ZOOM SECRETS!

1. Rehearse the future, just as it is desired, in your mind's eye.
2. Clearly see your desires in your mind's eye and believe they have materialized with feeling, belief and emotion.
3. Use your subconscious mind for solving problems by defining them and then writing down as many possible solutions as you can. Then hand the problem over to the subconscious mind — and forget it. Let the subconscious complete its computerized labor and hand over to you a Eureka! when it is ready. You must act on these Eurekas! when you receive them.
4. By gradually doing the things you fear, you will overcome fear. Let the subconscious warn you of impending danger.
5. Although you may be bogged down with all sorts of worries and problems you still must be enthusiastic. Act as though you are enthusiastic and the acting will turn into reality. Nothing great was ever achieved without enthusiasm.
6. "Act as if" in any circumstance you desire and it will be.
7. Cultivate the sixth sense by meditating in S.S.S. and also by living a bit more dangerously. Get yourself a motorcycle, take up mountaineering or anything else that will excite you and give you a tingle of adventure.

CHAPTER 3

THE SECRET OF GOALS

"Singleness of purpose is one of the chief essentials for success in life, no matter what may be one's aim."

JOHN D. ROCKEFELLER, JR.

All eyes are on the court, the tension mounts. The Harlem Globetrotters have the ball completely under control. With a magnificent flurry of arms and legs, the ball seems to come alive. A fancy dribble here, a pass there, the ball goes from one end of the court to the other, ready for the first shot. A Globetrotter still has the ball, the crowd is wild with anticipation. Half the crowd begins to shout simultaneously, "Shoot, shoot." But the dismayed player looks up in amazement. There is no net. How can he shoot? There is no goal to shoot at. The pantomime turns to pandemonium. There is confusion, frustration and resentment. The referee blows his whistle, the game is ended. You can't play basketball without goals, we all know that. You must have something to shoot at. You must have something to aim for.

When we don't have goals, we may decide to do something, but it proves difficult or we lose interest in it, so we move on to something else. We are like children in a toy shop grabbing one toy, letting it go and snatching another. In retrospect, we can see why we have not achieved success or accumulated money or done the things we should have done. We can see why we are not the people we ought to be. Our operative phrase has been, "give up, move on." If only we had some goals and persistently stuck to them, come what may, we would have achieved those goals.

To achieve success in any direction we must have goals. Let us look at the ways we can achieve goals. We have to know what to aim for and how long a period of time it will take to achieve our goals. Most people aim too low in life. Their failure to think big holds them back. If I gave you a dollar tomorrow and doubled it every day, how long would it take you to become a millionaire? It would happen like this: on the first day you would receive a dollar, on the second day two dollars, the third day four dollars, and so on, doubling up every day. Do you realize that in only twenty-one days you would be a millionaire? I know you will get out your pocket calculator, check and re-check the figures, but it's correct. I am not digressing; all of this is important. If you have $40,000 and invest it at only 7% per annum, within fifty years you would be a millionaire. Get your calculators out again and don't forget that the interest compounds. These calculations do disregard Uncle Sam, and his taxes, but their purpose is merely to show you how money can be generated. The point is people fail to attain their goals because they cannot visualize them.

The secret is to aim high. Then break your goals down into portions that can be visualized. You might find it hard to visualize actually being a millionaire. However, you should easily visualize having a chain of very small businesses each netting $250 a week. You only need sixteen small businesses netting $250 for four years to become a millionaire. Perhaps you can visualize sixteen salesmen each netting you $250 a week. Too many people fail through stupidity and through thinking in a constrained manner. They believe that with a positive mental attitude they can pull off

42

anything or walk through any mountain. I am not condemning positive thinking, but it is blind faith. Even the highest mountain can be climbed over, I agree, but if you are unskilled or unprepared you can fail. What you must do is break out of normal ways of thinking. Don't put boundaries on yourself and realize what you are, in fact, capable of doing. But temper that with what you can realistically achieve. Some things *are* impossible.

We have been discussing how the mystics, magis and fakirs of the East do incredible things by training and using their subconscious minds. History has it that a Tibetan mystic really believed that by training his subconscious mind he would become impervious to bullets. When he asked someone to test him, he was immediately shot dead. Again, recognize that some things are impossible!

People tend to give too short a period for the attainment of goals. The main reason for failure in these instances is simply that they are not visualizing properly. They set a time limit on a goal but fail to clearly visualize the goal and the time limit in their mind's eye. All they get is nothing or at best a foggy mess. You can set time limits if you are already in the habit of visualizing properly. If you are bringing into your possession the smaller things you desire through the practice of visualization then you are ready to set realistic time limits on larger objectives. However, if you're not visualizing small goals clearly and making them happen, you should not move on to bigger things. Start small and move up!

Because of the amount of research and study I have done in this field, I have had the happy experience of analysing my own successes and failures. It became obvious that the times I succeeded were the times I was visualizing clearly. The times I had failed, I had not been visualizing clearly. All I was getting was a haze. It became apparent that it was not the goals or the time limits I had set myself that caused the failure, but the fact that I had not been visualizing them clearly, concisely and regularly.

The subconscious mind is phenomenally powerful, but nevertheless it still takes time to assimilate and compute its plans. It needs a 21-day gestation period for a start, and it is essential that there be no breaks in it. It's no good to visualize for fifteen days and then miss a day. You would simply have to begin at the starting point again. Even when the 21-day period is complete, it is of the utmost importance that the visualizing is adhered to on the proper twice daily basis. This 21-day gestation period has a firm basis in psychology. Ask anyone who specializes in behaviour modification, they'll tell you it takes three weeks of concerted effort to break a habit or make something a habit.

To visualize well you must break down larger goals into parts you can comprehend. Hence a million dollars now becomes 1000 envelopes each containing 1000 dollars. In your imagination, see the money feel it believe it is in your possession, supercharge the atmosphere with emotion. It will be yours.

Deposit $10 in a new account and when your statement arrives, neatly type in another five zeros to make it a million dollars. Use this bank statement in, what should be, a twice daily visualizing routine. Use every little trick you can to stimulate your powerful subconscious mind into creativity.

Here is something from a Montaigne essay that tells the same story: "Fortis imaginatio generat casum." Translated, this means "A strong imagination begets the event."

When we examine it, we are not interested in earning a living. That really holds our interest from between 9 and 10 o'clock on Monday morning. No, we are interested in making a fortune, being someone, doing something extraordinary, possessing fantastic things. The best way to bring all this about is to have a list of goals. You actually require three lists of goals. The first is a list of the smaller things you require right now; the second is a list of your main goals and ambitions; and your third list contains one item only, your *definite chief aim*.

Let us say here and now that, once again, not thinking plays a large role in the organization of your list. Do not think whether or not you can acquire the goals of your desire — that is totally irrelevant. That you require and desire them is enough. Let's look at a chart of goals. You of course must decide what is to be on your own list. Until you can fill in all three categories, you are bound to fail. Until you can do this, you'll be like most other people. You'll go through life rudderless.

Normally when people read a book, any book, they tend to disregard charts; perhaps they think that they will come back to them later. Pay attention to this chart. Study it, fill it in with your own desires, goals and ambitions. Don't read another page until you have done this.

THINGS I WANT RIGHT NOW	MY AMBITIOUS GOALS	MY DEFINITE CHIEF AIM
Holiday	To own blue chip	To be a
Car serviced	stocks	millionaire
Bank loan paid	Porsche 982S	(or)
New stove	Rolls Royce	To be a film
House painted	To own a South	star
Dishwasher	Pacific Island	To be a presi-
New clothes	60 ft. yacht	dent of a
New colour T.V.	Winter home	corporation
Stereo equipment	Luxury world	(or)
Mink stole	cruise	Whatever it
Contact lenses	Be in control of	is you want
	my own profitable	as a *definite*
	business	*chief aim*

Now think about what you want — what *you* really want — and fill in this chart, your own chart. Although you must think about what you want, you don't have to think about how you will achieve these goals.

YOUR CHART

THINGS I WANT RIGHT NOW	MY AMBITIOUS GOALS	MY DEFINITE CHIEF AIM

Because of the way the subconscious mind works, it needs repetition of mental images. I consider it essential to have a scrapbook with pictures of all your desires pasted in it to help you with your visualizing program. Do this in the same manner of the man who desires a new car of a particular make and looks at it in the showroom every day. He'll get the color brochure on it and study it every night. This man is bound to attain the car. However, the man who just occasionally wishes he had a nicer car but does not believe he possibly can, or doesn't see it in his mind's eye, will surely not attain it.

Let us assume that one of the goals from your list is to own an expensive car. On the first page of your scrapbook you must commit that goal to writing. Do it in the *present* tense and in detail. It must be an accurate description of what you actually want; just writing down that you want a car is no good. The description should be something like:

> I own a brand new Rolls Royce convertible with an eight track stereo and magnesium alloy wheels. It is regal red with · beige interior and complete with telephone, cocktail cabinet and television.

If it is a Rolls Royce you want, fine. If it is a Porsche, Datsun or Mercedes you desire, write down its full description. On the page facing the description paste a picture of the car of your dreams. Do this with each and every one of your goals.

Now here is another secret. When you visualize the car, do not visualize the money aspect of it. The subconscious mind does not work like that. The business of the subconscious mind is to get you the car. It works like a computer, it analyses all your experiences, knows your past, present and future, takes inventory of your assets or lack of them, notes your environs, plots, plans, and creates the things you will have to do to achieve your goals. The plan may or may not include parting with money. The subconscious mind may prompt you to do something or other that will bring this goal about. It may seem to you perhaps the most illogical or even the most miraculous way. You might find yourself in a situation where you are given your car, meet someone who can help you get it, or you might have to do some small thing that will cause the car to come into your possession with little or no effort on your part.

But before all this, you must visualize clearly, with emotion, feeling and belief every night and every morning. Second, do not think about how you will achieve the objective during the rest of the day. Again, the subconscious mind needs no help from you in the creation of its plans. Visualize any goal you require, be it material possessions or an intangible achievement. Visualization is the key you must use to engage the powerful subconscious mind in successful creative operation. Visualization is cleverly encapsulated in this little verse:

> If you can see it, you can be it!
> If you can see it, you can do it!
> If you can see it, you can have it!

When you visualize your Rolls Royce, feel and smell the genuine leather upholstered interior; feel the grain of the walnut instrument panel; touch that smooth exterior; listen to that big V8 engine pull silently as only a Rolls Royce can do; sit in it; drive it; see the car; feel thrilled that you are driving it — you must believe you own it. The powerful subconscious mind is bound by psychological law to provide a foolproof Eureka! for its attainment. To reiterate, it is no good having a list of goals and reading them out like a parrot every night and every morning. That will achieve precisely nothing. The goals must be clearly and accurately written down in the present tense and visualized with emotion, belief and feeling; then you must not think about them until your next visualization session. Never worry that anyone else might beat you to your goals; this is a particularly common but unfounded fear. There is more than one of everything. Even if someone brings out an idea you have thought of before you do, there is no cause for concern. Competition only generates more business. The subconscious mind must be given time to assimilate the facts and your desires. Genius never hurries and everything takes the time it takes. It's easy to become impatient as we wait for the subconscious mind to hand over its next illuminating plan or idea. You must be patient. Eurekas! from the subconscious mind are plans worth waiting for because they are always foolproof.

In visualizing your goals you must rely on your own creative subconscious mind to come up with the idea or plan for the attainment of your goals. That is why you do not specify in what capacity you will make your money or attain your goals. It is the job of the subconscious mind to provide these plans. All you should do is follow through with whatever the subconscious mind tells you to do.

You must visualize exactly what you require — near enough is not good enough. Don't be like the man who half-heartedly wanted an exotic fishpond in his garden. He didn't see it clearly enough. One day to his surprise his neighbour knocked on the door and handed him a fishbowl with two scraggly goldfish in it. The neighbour was leaving the area but did not want to take the fish with him. You see, in the past the neighbour had probably picked up on the fact that the guy next door had said something about fish! If our subject had clearly visualized a pond in the garden with exotic fish in it, the very same psychological laws would have made it happen.

Another one of the goals from your list may be a dream house. In your scrapbook write down its full description *as though you already own it*. On the facing page paste a picture of the exact house you want. If your dream house has four bathrooms, two pools, and a sauna and tennis courts, make sure they all get written down in the description and appear in the picture.

Another goal of yours may be to own a diamond ring or a certain piece of jewellery or a kitchen fitted with every conceivable modern appliance. Write down full descriptions and paste the appropriate pictures on the facing pages. For the pictures cut up mail-order catalogues, manufacturer's brochures, travel agency promotional material, photographs from magazines, anything that clearly depicts what you want will do. It is important to have a complete written statement in the present tense and a corresponding picture in your scrapbook for you to visualize with.

Here's another secret. Buy a little something for the goal you want to come about. For example, say you are visualizing a dream house, buy a little of the curtain material you intend to use, or some kitchen utensils for your new kitchen. For the car of your dreams buy some tools or a can of turtle wax or a steering-wheel cover.

These positive affirmations sink deep into the subconscious mind and speed up the Eureka! experience. Let's imagine that one of your goals is to see relatives abroad. Well, buy some new suitcases to confirm to your subconscious that you intend to go. Perhaps a 60-foot yacht is on your list, buy a compass and some maps of the waterways you intend to travel. If some stereo equipment is your desire, buy a tape or your favorite album. Use every psychological tool at your disposal to get the subconscious mind into operation.

Now that we have the basics of visualization down, I want to expand my example of how the subconscious mind works. It concerns some of the flashes of inspiration I have had, the Eurekas! that come from the subconscious mind. I left school at the age of fourteen and started work in the construction industry. The work was hard, really hard and the pay was low, really low. Although I didn't realize it at the time, I was visualizing. I held a picture in my mind's eye of being loaded with money. In a very short time I had my first Eureka! It came to me in a flash. On the various building sites there were always scraps of metal lying around. My brilliant idea was to regularly collect the scrap, which consisted of copper and lead pipes and brass water pump fittings. I began to sell the scrap and in no time at all the revenue generated from the scrap business exceeded that of my weekly wage from the building trade.

My hobby was racing motorcycles and every evening I spent hours tuning and building racing engines in the silence and solitude of my workshop, which was in the depths of the countryside. You must understand that at that time I did not appreciate the significance of S.S.S. or visualization.

The construction work was literally killing me. Some of the prefabricated panels weighed over 250 pounds and working with those every day was no joke. I still kept a picture in my mind's eye of being a successful and wealthy man. I had another Eureka! that came to me while I wasn't thinking. I decided to quit working for the construction company that was employing me, go it alone and collect all the profits for myself. I did this with great success, although the work was still as hard and heavy as ever, but at least the financial reward was my own.

Perhaps I am a bit slow, but the significance of the circumstances in which I had had my flashes of inspiration, which occurred *while* I was getting periods of silence, stillness and solitude and *because* I was visualizing, still hadn't dawned on me.

I enthusiastically carried on in the evenings in my quiet workshop when suddenly I had another Eureka! This time it was a brilliant idea, and the course of my life altered dramatically as I followed it through. The idea was to quit the construction industry altogether and set up shop selling motorcycles.

Although at the time I didn't understand the power of the subconscious mind I did have an overwhelming gut feeling that I must go out and look for suitable premises. I knew intuitively that I would find just what I was looking for. At the time, I put down what subsequently happened to luck, fate and my good fortune. My subconscious guided me to a shop that had previously been used as a motorcycle showroom. Within two weeks I had rented the shop from the landlord, who had retired from selling motorcycles. The next problem was how to fill the showroom with stock without any capital expenditure. I didn't really consider it a problem, because I knew somehow or other I could fill the place with machines. That's exactly what I saw in my mind's eye: a showroom full of motorcycles. Lo and behold, while quietly sweeping out my workshop I had the Eureka! All I had to do was telephone the hundreds of individuals who were trying to sell their bikes privately through classified ads. I would put them in the showroom and offer them to the public with financing and insurance available. For my efforts, I would take a percentage of the asking price. This is known as selling on consignment. Invariably I got more than the asking price so I kept the over and above profit as well. The scheme worked so well that in a short period of time I had seven extremely profitable shops all operating without capital investment.

Obviously this story is a condensed version of what happened over a number of years. I don't want you to get the impression that Eurekas! come daily. What I do want to impress upon you is that if you visualize your desires and get periods of S.S.S. the Eurekas! will come along. All you have to do is follow them through to their logical conclusion.

At the time I had the motorcycle shops I began to diversify vast amounts of money into many projects. Unfortunately things began to go wrong. It was around this time that the truth about S.S.S. and visualization dawned on me; in fact the dawning was yet another Eureka! You could say that I had a Eureka! about Eurekas! I discovered the S.S.S. formula and the visualization tactics and how they worked. It was just as well, because by this time I was at my wits end.

However, once I decided what I was about and what I wanted out of life I managed to gather it all up again. By this time of course I was deliberately taking time out to meditate in S.S.S. and to visualize my desires and goals.

Once I had grasped the potential of the S.S.S. formula and the power of visualization, things really started to happen. I got into business consulting, property development and buying and selling just about every conceivable commodity, idea and service. I also learned the way to sell was by talking.

This example clearly shows that my subconscious mind was working out plans for my goals without me even knowing it. When I stumbled on how the subconscious mind did work, I really delved into it deeply and that was an interesting and profitable exercise in itself. The philosophy presented in this book is the outcome.

By understanding how it works you have more than a head start on the rest of the field. You are probably beginning to see that in order to achieve your goals a number of things are necessary to bring the subconscious mind into operation so that it can provide the correct plan.

Action is a very important ingredient, so much so that I have devoted a complete chapter to action. However, I will make the introduction to it in this chapter.

Years ago I heard G. K. Chesterton's words, that "Everyone on earth should believe that he has something to give the world which cannot otherwise be given." I did believe this, although at the same time I did not know what I could contribute to the world. Now the following story concerns me and my contribution, and the point of the story is to demonstrate that it is necessary to get into action with the tools and ideas you already have at your disposal. By meditating and visualizing regularly the subconscious mind will take over, and when you are not thinking it will hand over devastatingly illuminating plans for success. Here is my story:

I decided that my contribution to the world would be a motivational book based on my personal business experience. I desired that my book would be an all-time best seller, and I would be a resounding success as a self-help author. Every night and every morning I visualized the same thing. I saw my book in bookstores and being ordered through the mail. I saw huge orders coming in from major sales companies. I was in bookshops all over the country personally autographing copies of my book. I was being interviewed on hundreds of television and radio shows throughout America. I saw all this in my mind's eye. I got into action and started to write. The book was called *The Psychology Behind Success and Selling*. I wrote page after page, chapter after chapter. I wasn't by any means pleased, but I kept on writing. Throughout my business career I have always visualized my goals and ambitions. The book I was writing was no different from any other business undertaking. I knew that after a period of time, the subconscious mind would unfold its plan, so I carried on writing. I got as far as saying that whatever our vocation, we all live by selling something, and the way we sell is by talking. I had such chapters as "The Power of Words," "The Power of Partnerships," "The Power to Please," "The Power of Contracts," and so on and so forth. Much of what I wrote would not have inspired even the most desperate student of success. Most of what I wrote was painfully boring, but I kept going.

Then suddenly while not thinking, when I least expected it, my subconscious mind unfolded its Eureka! "Why call your book *The Psychology Behind Success and Selling*? A much better title is *TALK AND GROW RICH*!" With the title came an idea for the cover, which I immediately drew out and visualized on. Now I had the title and the cover design. The more I meditated and visualized, the more the subconscious mind unfolded to me. "The Power of Words" became "The Orator Is King," "The Power of Partnerships" became "Man Power". More and more occurred to me as each chapter progressed. As I wasn't thinking, the plan unfolded itself. The content of each chapter was altered and I can honestly say that none of the original material I wrote ended up in this book. All, and I mean all, of the good ideas, titles, stories, plots and plans came while I wasn't thinking. Most important is that every night I visualized the success of the book. I could see it as a best seller and I believed it. I regularly meditated in S.S.S., and I got into action with the tools and ideas I had used in the beginning. Without making a start the subconscious mind would have had nothing to work with.

Even the most zealous apprentice millionaire would have a task cut out for himself trying to achieve his definite chief aim in one fell swoop. You must learn how to break down larger objectives into smaller ones. Roger Bannister, the first man to break a four-minute mile, did so by breaking down his main goal. He broke down the mile into four quarters of a full mile. He would dash off a quarter mile in 58 seconds or less and then jog the rest of the way. Bannister trained not only his body but also his mind. He held the picture of the first four-minute mile in his mind, it was his predominant thought. He trained his mind by taking up mountain climbing. This taught him persistence and how to overcome any obstacle that got in his way. When Bannister ran his great race on May 6, 1954, he joined four of his quarter mile goals together and ran the mile in 3 minutes 59.6 seconds.

Going back even further, to the days of old in England, when knights in shining armor and castles were commonplace, history has it that a knight gambled with the local gentry, peasants and royalty that he could jump to the top of a castle. Everyone bet what they could afford and on the great day, thousands turned up to see this spectacular feat. How could this be done, they thought? Witchcraft, sorcery, magic? The knight was ready, his armour glistening in the sun. He placed his two feet together and jumped *one step at a time* right up the spiral staircase to the top of the castle.

The subconscious mind will know exactly what is necessary for you to do in order for you to succeed in your endeavours. Providing that you take time out in S.S.S. for meditation and regularly practice visualization, the subconscious mind will, step by step, reveal the plan in order for you to reach your goal. And that's how you must undertake the plan, step by step.

Keep in touch with your subconscious. Now that you are visualizing regularly and getting daily periods of S.S.S. the subconscious will tell you many things. You might feel prompted to buy a certain book or visit a certain person in an office. Perhaps you will get an urge to make a phone call or look through some newspaper advertisements that you normally avoid. At the time, some of the things the subconscious mind will tell you to do will seem illogical, carry them out immediately and exactly as the subconscious told you to. Only when you have achieved your goal will you be able to trace the things your subconscious mind has told you to do and see how they formed a chain of logical events and actions.

Pour the wine and cut the cake when you realize the truth behind the old but misunderstood statement that "thoughts are things." Conscious thoughts are no such thing, they merely clutter up one's mind in the form of incessant chatter, untruths, worries and are unnecessary. Conscious thoughts are the internal dialogue that we have discussed at great length and taken great pains to stop. Conscious thoughts are hobgoblins! The thoughts that come while not thinking come as a result of computer-like labour from the subconscious mind. *These thoughts are truly things.* The thoughts that come from the subconscious mind are *Eurekas*!

You can pat yourself on the back when you realize the truth behind the equally old saying, "Necessity is the mother of invention." By following this philosophy, you will make it absolutely necessary for your subconscious mind to invent.

One extremely important point I want to make: there are three main systems we use in our complex internal cognitive processes. Put simply, we can visualize in our mind's eye (visual), we can talk within ourselves and hear voices in our minds (auditory), and we can have feelings and emotions (kinesthetic). We all use each of these systems to one degree or another, but there is an important catch. Each one of us uses *one* of these systems more than the other two. That creates problems! The problems are many — but the problem I want to discuss with you now is that of visualizing. A person who is visual can visualize his goals in his mind's eye all day long — he has no problem. But what of those who are auditory and kinesthetic? They might have a problem seeing pictures of their goals in their minds' eye. The problem is easily overcome once you are aware that it is a problem. If you are auditory (you talk and listen within yourself a lot) or if you are kinesthetic (you feel and have emotions about things a lot) then, when you visualize, try as hard as you can to see your goals in your mind's eye — but also use the process you do normally. Practice makes perfect.

No matter whether your thought processes are visual, auditory or kinesthetic you must use all the processes when you visualize, because as well as the visual picture in your mind's eye, feeling emotion and telling yourself that you are going to achieve your goals counts for everything.

One final point: never forget that there are three systems of internal processes — namely, visual, auditory and kinesthetic, and that we all use all of the processes, but that nevertheless each of us uses *one* more than the other two.

Later you will be astonished to see where else this is going to help you in your apprenticeship!

ZOOM SECRETS!

1. Draw up a list of goals — the things you want right now, your ambitious goals and your definite chief aim. Don't wonder if you can achieve them or not — that you desire them is sufficient.
2. Write each goal down in precise detail, in the present tense, and put this description next to the picture of the goal in a scrapbook.
3. To make your scrapbook, cut up mail order catalogues, magazines, travel brochures, promotional material — anything at all that shows exactly what you desire.
4. Look through this scrapbook every night and every morning with the feeling, emotion and belief that your goals have already materialized.
5. After you have been visualizing for a length of time it is inevitable that your subconscious mind will produce Eurekas!(foolproof success ideas), and it is of essence that you carry these out immediately and to the letter.
6. Buy a little "something" toward your goal. For your dream house you might buy a door knocker, for your car some tools and for your yacht maybe a map or a compass. Use every psychological tool at your disposal to engage the subconscious into creativity.
7. The subconscious mind will give you many small promptings to enable you to attain your goals. Some of these promptings may seem illogical, but nevertheless carry them out to the letter. Only when you have achieved your goal will you be able to trace your steps back and see how right the subconscious was.
8. If you are kinesthetic or auditory you will have to try particularly hard in order to visualize your goals. Use your own system as well. Practice makes perfect.

CHAPTER 4

THE ORATOR IS KING

*"I see that everywhere among the race of men,
it is the tongue that wins not the deed."*

SOPHOCLES

In the foregoing chapters we have discovered how to solve problems, clear up inhibitions and, most important of all, how to stop the internal dialogue to enable us to hear the Eurekas! from the subconscious mind.

It becomes obvious, now, that whenever a Eureka! presents itself you have to get into action. The fact that is often overlooked is that talking is the main ingredient for converting Eurekas! into money.

On numerous occasions I have been called into various businesses as a consultant and, in the final analysis, all the problems I encountered could have been solved if more of the end product had been sold. I could also name well over a thousand individuals who have basements overflowing with one item or another which they either invested in to resell or had manufactured themselves in the hope of making their fortunes. It is not only the large corporations that need to let the scales fall from their eyes, but anyone who is involved in the great game of making money.

Many a manufacturer has come to grief due to his false belief that if he produces the best in quality, and his goods are competitively priced, they will automatically sell. Unfortunately this is not the way of the world; it is far from the truth. Even the best, the cheapest, the brightest and the most ingenious goods still have to be sold.

For many years successful businessmen have recognized that the salesman is the kingpin of industry. With such an abundance of goods chasing so few people, it is a buyers' market. Manufacturers spend not millions, but billions, of dollars annually on advertising to promote and sell their wares. Even with this expenditure it is still the competitor who can train and motivate fleets of competent salesmen to actually go out and sell who dominates the market. Take note of the sales forces of Mary Kay Cosmetics, Tupperware, The Combined Insurance Company of America and the Amway Corporation.

"Nothing happens until somebody sells something." The expression may be trite but it is still true. Selling is the denominator of industrial growth. Let us remember that the factory that does not sell its goods soon goes out of business. If a factory goes out of business, people lose their jobs, and along with their jobs, their livelihoods. People on the shop floor, the machinists, wage clerks, draftsmen, typists, secretaries, sweepers and toolmakers, to the staff in managerial positions, executives, and presidents of companies all lose their jobs. They are all dependent on the salesmen selling the end product, whether it be goods, services or ideas. No sales means no jobs.

Before we even consider the spoken word used in conjunction with selling or used to *Talk and Grow Rich*, we must be absolutely certain in our minds as to whether the spoken word is, or is not, powerful.

Just for a moment consider three of the most powerful words in the world, "I love you." These words are nothing short of magic and can lift the recipient on to a new plane of living, they can revitalize marriages, make old folk young, give people reason to live, turn sadness into happiness, tears into laughter, mediocrity into genius and cause fatigue to fall away. No matter how long a couple have been married, and even if they have lived together with everything in the relationship in harmony, without these words spoken frequently they are not living, they are just existing. Oh so many couples take each other for granted these days. No wonder things often turn sour. Even with all the little gifts, dinner out and other material things, with no spoken word, something is sadly lacking.

Consider the words, "I am sorry." Again, only three words, but if they are used in the right place they can transform relationships, friendships, partnerships and marriages. People's pride stops them from using these three words, and it is this pride that keeps them from achieving power, for the power is in the spoken word. What has all this got to do with making money, you ask? Well, I will tell you. If you cannot sell yourself to your nearest and dearest, how on earth do you expect to sell yourself to the big wide world?

When we study the annals of wars, revolutions and campaigns for this "ism" and that "ism," we soon discover that the great leaders are the great orators. Do you think that you can get men worked up to such a degree that they will act totally against their most powerful emotion — self-preservation — and actually go to war and fight, even risk being killed by thinking great thoughts, or even by writing them letters explaining the situation with pictures in technicolor, or by sending them glossy highly colored pictorial brochures with captions explaining the action? NO! But we find that the *spoken* word has the power to lift kind, loving and peaceful men up from one country and put them down in another, hating, fighting and killing.

Most people consider themselves forward to a certain degree in frank and straightforward talking. We are not. Many people still suffer from acute shyness. This seems especially true in cities with dense populations. In New York or London, for example, strangers almost never speak to each other.

Once I met a youth coming out of a dance looking very dejected. "How many girls did you dance with?" I asked. "None," was the reply. "Well, how many did you ask to dance?" I queried. Again the reply was "None." You may laugh, or you may inwardly realize that many people go through their whole lives not talking, not asking.

Let us take a community like that of the Lake District in England. People walking down the street acknowledge one another, people sitting next to each other on a train or bus will automatically converse with each other. Although these people meet strangers all the time, they still talk to them. You see, although the people in the Lake District may be strangers to one another, but they have been born and bred there. Now that is not the case in New York or London or, for that matter, in any other very large city. The population is transient. It is instead more common for children to be brought up on doctrines like, "Don't speak to strangers," "Mind your own business," and generally to think in a manner not congenial to making friends easily. Many people think like this: "If he's just passing through and I will only talk to him for a few brief minutes, why bother?" How many times have you spoken to anyone on a train or a bus? How many people do you know who don't even talk to their neighbours? The foregoing may be all right in itself, but we find that when we want to talk to somebody, we are unable to. We have been practicing not talking all our lives. In Germany they have a proverb, "Education begins a gentleman, conversation completes him," and Erasmus wrote "By speaking men learn to speak."

Consider the times that you personally have had really good ideas. You feel they are good and that they are exactly what you want to do, but you still have to coax and persuade other people, with the spoken word, to go along with your plans. Whichever way you look at it, you find that all the professional persuaders, including great leaders, politicians and salesmen use the spoken word to convince, sway, motivate, procure, persuade, inspire and sell. Whichever way you look at it, the Orator Is King.

You say you don't like talking, you are shy and always say the wrong things at the wrong time. You think it is going to be too much trouble, you don't think you can persuade people to go along with your ideas, or buy your products. Emerson knew this and it prompted him to say, "All the great speakers were bad speakers at first." And Samuel Johnson said, "Nothing will ever be attempted if all possible objections must first be overcome." I think you will like talking. I also know the effort involved is going to pay handsome dividends. Go forward with a splendid heart.

Generally speaking, the most successful people in selling, whether they are selling goods, ideas or services, are not necessarily gifted with fluency. They may not have what we might call the "gift of gab." Usually the competent salesman does have a sort of charisma. However if you have not got this charisma now, you certainly will have it by the time you have finished this book. Carefully incorporated in this book is all the knowledge that you require to *Talk and Grow Rich*.

Vittorio Orlando wrote, "Oratory is just like prostitution; you must have little tricks." It is these little tricks that I will endeavor to show you in the coming chapters. But before I show you any little tricks I feel there is one big trick you ought to know about.

The trick, the one trick that separates the star salesman from the amateur has nothing to do with whether he is fat or thin, short or tall. It has nothing to do with how he gets his leads or finds his prospects. The big trick all star salesmen have in common is this: *They transact their sale in a conversational manner, they sell themselves to other people, and they sell something that is good value for money, be it product or service.*

The amateur salesman rushes in and tries hard to make a sale. He uses all the high pressure tactics he knows. What happens is that the prospect realizes he is being sold and freezes up. Invariably he doesn't buy. The Apprentice Millionaire will conduct a sales transaction without his prospect even realizing that a sale is taking place at all. The customer buys without even realizing he is being sold. In fact, he *buys* as distinct from his *being sold*! "Ours is the country where in order to sell your product," wrote Louis Kronenberger, "you don't so much point out the merits as you first work like hell to sell yourself."

Let's go back to the big trick that all successful salesmen use, because this is a very important point. I made very certain to tell you what they did and I made equally certain not to tell you how they do it. It's a frightening and fascinating fact that thousands of successful salesmen use these components, but that they themselves don't realize what they are doing. Many even write books about selling, but miss *all* the important points, because what they are doing is something they do subconsciously!

Incidentally, the term I use most frequently in this book is "salesman." When I do, I mean "salesman" in the broadest possible sense. It saves the use of cumbersome devices such as "salesperson" or "he and she." However, please remember that selling and success know no boundaries for the sexes. We are all salesmen. As Robert Louis Stevenson said, "We all live by selling something."

Your Eureka! experience will be a foolproof idea. Nevertheless, it is imperative that you know how to sell it in order to convert it into money. Some of the most brilliant ideas in the world nearly didn't get off the ground until they were sold properly. Typical of these brilliant ideas was "Monopoly," one of the most successful games ever invented. For years no one was interested in the Xerox copying machine. Edison even had to light a complete house, free of charge, before anyone would listen to him about the future possibilities of the electric light. When Walter Hunt and Elias Howe invented the sewing machine, they, too, had a job convincing people that it was practical.

Once again: nothing happens until somebody sells something. Andrew Carnegie recognized this truth and it prompted him to say, "You can take away my factories and my money, but leave my salesmen — and I will be back to where I am today in less than two years." Which prompts me to say again, "The Orator Is King!"

ZOOM SECRETS!

1. A fact often overlooked is that talking is the main ingredient for converting Eurekas! into money. Remember nothing happens until somebody sells something!

2. Do not underestimate the power of the spoken word. It is one of the most important methods used by great leaders, politicians and salesmen to convince, sway, motivate, persuade and sell.

3. No-one will dance with you if you don't ask. You can't even take your own spouse out to the theatre if you don't ask, and you certainly won't sell anything if you don't ask.

4. The big trick all star salesmen have in common is this: they transact their sale in a conversational manner. They sell themselves to other people, and they sell something that is a good value for money, be it product or service. Whether they know how or why they do this remains to be seen. A little later on you will see that many successful salesmen do something of which they themselves are completely unaware. This is the true secret of success!

CHAPTER 5

TALK AND GROW RICH

"To talk is our chief business in this world, and talk is by far the most accessible pleasure. It costs nothing in money; it is all profit, it completes education, founds and fosters friendships, and can be enjoyed at any age and in almost any state of health."

ROBERT LOUIS STEVENSON

We are painstakingly analysing the power of the spoken word. Its simplicity is likely to cause you to overlook its potential.

Let me say here and now that people can be divided into three groups (the population per group is irrelevant for this observation). The first group consists of those to whom anyone can sell anything and who will believe anything. They are the gullible suckers. The second group does think about what they are buying, but when they come up against a topflight salesman, they will usually succumb. They are the Mr. Averages, nice guys, genuine people. And last, but by no means least, we have the know-it-alls. You can't tell them anything. This is the group who falls hardest. It happens so quickly that they never even see it coming. In this group you have the person who says he never takes any notice of television commercials or any form of advertising. Little do these people realize that the multi-billion dollar advertising industry is geared to exactly that kind of thinking and that every manufactured article is wrapped, coloured and priced in such a psychologically knowledgeable and subliminal way as to induce them to buy. Even supermarkets are geared for selling to the know-it-alls. The width of the aisles, the size of the shopping carts, the height of the grocery shelves, the color of the cans, the lighting, the heating, the Muzak, everything, every last detail, is geared to make the know-it-alls spend money. And you know something? They do!

When you *Talk and Grow Rich* you come up against all these types of people, including the know-it-alls. When you do, even the know-it-alls won't pose a problem to you because dynamic psychology was specifically devised for selling to such people. For even the most demanding and sophisticated buyer there is no haven. With dynamic psychology you get below the buyer's threshold of consciousness in such a subtle way that your selling is not even perceived.

When you *Talk and Grow Rich* you convert your Eurekas! into their monetary equivalent. Notice I say *your* Eurekas! It is very important when reading a book like this that you read between the lines and see how you can utilize each sales story and each example in your own daily life. When you *Talk and Grow Rich*, the sky is the limit! Read between the lines of the next two or three inspiring stories and see how you can apply them in your own life.

Probably the greatest success story of the last century has been told many times. Unfortunately, in my opinion, the *secret* of its success has never really been made clear. I refer to the conception and formation of the United States Steel Corporation.

To get a clear picture it is necessary to indulge in some fantasy. Take yourself back to the evening of the twelfth of December, 1900. You are in the banquet hall of the University Club on Fifth Avenue in New York. Among the guests are the rich of the time, J. W. Gates, the Stillmans, the Harrimans, the Vanderbilts, and the

Emperor of Wall Street and renowned financier, John Pierpont Morgan. Also present is a certain Charles M. Schwab, Andrew Carnegie's company president. The lavish eight course banquet is being thrown for Mr. Schwab by J. Edward Simmons and Charles Stewart Smith in return for kindness Schwab has bestowed on them at previous conventions. Imagine yourself in that banquet hall, with eighty millionaires, whose total net worth is probably over five billion dollars.

Having consumed the lobster, caviar, consommé and roast veal, and having finished the sumptuous eighth course, you are served brandy. Cigars are lit. The speeches begin.

Nothing dramatic happens until it is Charles Schwab's turn. He is expected to grace the table for a few moments with polite but meaningless vapour. But he doesn't. Instead he stampedes the convention with a one-and-a-half-hour speech. He speaks of the disorganization of the steel industry, the competition and the cut-throating, the duplication of mills and loss of profits. He speaks of overheads and administrative departments and the capturing of foreign markets. He puts forward a plan that will amalgamate them all in one huge profitable trust. There will be no duplication, just one huge trust that runs the steel industry from start to finish.

Charles M. Schwab hypnotized those eighty millionaires with his eloquence and the clear-cut program he laid down for the amalgamation of the steel industry. The United States Steel Corporation was thus conceived. Money-master Morgan agreed in principle to undertake the huge operation of floating the company by organizing money from the stock market in order to bring the corporation into being. Even he wondered if Schwab could persuade the canny wee Scot, Andrew Carnegie, to sell his steel interests — and if he did, for how much? Morgan knew that the Carnegie business, due to its enormous size, had to come under the tent of the newly conceived United States Steel Corporation. For, without it, the trust would be a farce, and as one writer put it, "A plum pudding without the plums."

As it happened, Schwab did persuade his boss to sell. He used the same hypnotic eloquence and the same silver-tongued loquaciousness he used on the eighty millionaires at the University Club banquet hall. Schwab poured out glittering promises of untold millions, of luxury cruises and retirement in euphoria. Carnegie's price? Four hundred million dollars.

By the time the steel mills were brought into legal existence, the value of the properties had increased by an estimated six-hundred million dollars. Morgan and the others made millions of dollars in excess profits, Schwab was made president of the newly founded steel company and he remained in control until 1930.

Charles M. Schwab's speech and the way he conveyed it to the minds of all those concerned was marketed for a profit of $600,000,000. Not an insignificant amount for a single after-dinner speech!

Let us consider an alternative method of communicating to those eighty millionaires about the proposed amalgamation. Schwab could have written them letters, or sent them glossy folders with the facts and the proposition neatly plotted out so they could read it through and be thrilled with the projected profits. But no! It just would not work. The galvanic force and effect needed to convince and motivate those bankers, brokers and industrialists could only be found in the spoken word! *There was no other way Schwab could have sold the idea to J.P. Morgan and the others on that night of December 12th, 1900. Men really do talk and grow rich!*

Nor would there be a better way of doing such a deal today — because men really do *Talk and Grow Rich.*

The secret behind the profitable deal just outlined

can hardly be considered a secret anymore. The talking done by Charles Schwab to those eighty millionaires was done in a conversational manner. At the same time he sold himself to them. Schwab knew exactly what he was about. He even once said, "We are all salesmen, every day of our lives. We are selling our ideas, our plans, our energies, our enthusiasms, to those with whom we come in contact. Thus the man of genial personality is bound to accomplish more than the man without it."

Consider for a moment that vast money making cosmetic company, Avon. In 1973, this company was worth more on the stock market than the entire United States steel industry. All this due to the efforts of the thousands of Avon salespeople, all of whom *Talk and Grow Rich*. And they've made not only themselves rich, but have made Avon one of the most profitable companies in the U.S.A.

Do not be dismayed by the enormous size of the foregoing businesses. It is all too easy to miss the crucial points being made. When a person has no capital, no ideas and no assets it is difficult to see how such examples can relate to his or her own particular dreams. All I will say for the moment is that if you want to set up an empire similar to Avon's, there is nothing in the world that will stop you from doing it. Complete instructions are in this book. You don't even need capital!

Muhammed Ali, one of the world's greatest celebrities, has earned a reputed thirty-four million dollars from boxing. He is a legend in his own lifetime and a world-wide household name. No one will deny that he is a fantastic boxer, but what has made him that rich? Yes, his brilliance as an orator! Take away the pre-fight oratory and ask yourself if all the little old ladies downtown would watch him. All the hundreds of millions of world-wide television viewers, the majority of whom are not even interested in boxing, would they want to watch skillful boxing for the sake of it! Never! People love to hear the eloquence, the showmanship, the loquaciousness. That is the best and most exciting part. Ali is a good boxer, the best, but even the very best still have to be sold! Ali's verbal talents have done more for boxing than anything since the beginning of the sport.

The stage is set, or perhaps, in this instance, I should say the ring. The greatest heavyweight champion in the history of boxing is in one corner; in the other, who knows? It is of little consequence. Ali starts his oratory.

"Look at you; fat, ugly, Oh so slow, slow, slow, slow, Why chump I betcha scare yourself to death just staring in the mirror. You ugly bear, you ain't never fought nobody but tramps and has-beens." The atmosphere is electric, it could be cut with a knife. The prize purse is a record, the box office take, another. The crowd is ecstatic or hysterical, probably both. "Float like a butterfly, sting like a bee, your hands can't hit what your eyes can't see." Some folks are booing, others are cheering. Some love him, others hate him. "I've rassled with an alligator, I've tussled with a whale, I've done handcuffed lighnin', and thrown thunder in jail. I'm the greatest, am I immortal?" The boxer takes off the sandwich board-type placard that reads, "Psychological Warfare" and he is ready to fight.

You too, can *Talk and Grow Rich* no matter what your vocation or ultimate goal. The principles are contained herein, all you have to do is to use them. Many of you will have read Napoleon Hill's celebrated masterpiece, *Think and Grow Rich*. I got, and still get, a tremendous amount out of it. Hill's book sold well over five-million copies. Where lies the secret of Hill's success? Surely the secret lies in the talking. Witness the interviews he had with over five hundred of the most prominent and successful men in America, men of the caliber of Ford, Rockefeller, Edison, Woolworth, Burbank, Darrow, Morgan, Firestone, Wanamaker, Wilson, Randolph and Roosevelt. Can you honestly say that Napoleon Hill could have produced a book like his without those interviews? If Napoleon Hill had not been personable his original interview with Andrew Carnegie would not have borne judgment, let alone an introduction to America's wealthiest and greatest. Nor would Carnegie have "tossed" him the secret of success or implanted the idea in Hill's head about giving a success philosophy to the world. We might never have had Hill's success philosophy had Carnegie not been taken with Hill's loquaciousness and personality. Napoleon Hill had to be personable, garrulous, and effective. He was a conversationalist, an orator. No "interviews," no book. You are also beginning to see that all men, even writers and journalists, *Talk and Grow Rich*.

In the last few years authors have promoted their books in the typical *Talk and Grow Rich* tradition. Og Mandino gave forty-nine radio and television interviews, as well as interviews to over two dozen newspaper reporters when he promoted his million copy best seller, *The Greatest Salesman in the World*.

Dr. Wayne W. Dyer covered over 28,000 miles promoting his book, *Your Erroneous Zones*, and in doing so saw 48 of the 50 states and gave over 700 radio and television interviews. Dr. Dyer inadvertently used the *Talk and Grow Rich* philosophy to promote his remarkable book onto the best seller list.

The founding president of Temple University, Dr. Russell H. Conwell, used six-million dollars of his own money to establish the institution. The money came from the proceeds of his fabulous and awe-inspiring lecture, "Acres of Diamonds." This lecture was given some 6000 times to millions of people. The main theme of the lecture was to inspire men and women to do great things with their lives, not miles away in far and distant lands, but in their own backyards. In his lectures he graphically illustrated, time and time again, how people fail to recognize the potential of fame and fortune at their feet. When these very same people can't see the forest for the trees, they are all too anxious to move on in search of their fortunes, only to learn, dismayed, that they had left their fortunes behind them. Dr. Conwell, unknowingly, used dynamic psychology when he delivered his lecture. He would arrive in town early on the day of the lecture, sometimes even the night before. He then made it his business to get some background about the people of that town. Dr. Conwell would talk to housewives, ministers, doctors, factory workers, school children, teachers and the townsfolk in general. He would find out their desires, their ideals, their ambitions, the advantages they had and the opportunities they had failed to recognize. By the time he had finished his mini-market survey, he was ready to get up on the rostrum and deliver his sermon. He adapted the principles of his lecture to suit the people of each town. He pointed out the "Acres of Diamonds" in their own backyards, and he generated millions of dollars by talking.

When you consider all the cases you have just read you soon realize that no matter how brilliant the idea or product, the only way to sell it, successfully, is with the spoken word. The spoken word has power and persuasiveness. But, more importantly for you, it can be personalized and directed. However, remember, you could not tape the spoken word of a salesman and send it out on tapes or records to sell your goods, for, as I have already pointed out, the secret lies in a "conversational manner." That requires person-to-person contact. The written word simply is not effective enough. Anyone who has done a "direct mail shot" or a "leaflet drop" knows — the return can be dismal.

The potential for anyone wishing to *Talk and Grow Rich* is nothing short of phenomenal simply because every manufactured article around you, inside and outside the home, in the hobby shop and in the street has to be sold, not just once, but many times. The foregoing is true also of the office equipment you use, the office itself, the car that gets you to the office and the gasoline the car uses. Originally the ideas behind these things had to be sold, and when the idea had been converted into reality, it had to be sold again from the manufacturer to the distributor to the wholesaler to the retailer and to the consumer. You can imagine the selling, hence the talking, that takes place on the long route from drawing board to consumer.

Remember, there is not a money-making deal that does not revolve around talking!

ZOOM SECRETS!

1. With dynamic psychology you can sell to the gullible suckers, the genuine people, even to the know-it-alls. It happens so quickly they never see it coming, because your selling is way below their threshold of consciousness.
2. When Charles Schwab sold the idea for amalgamating the steel industry, he used the spoken word. Today as well, that would be the only conceivable way of selling such a deal.
3. It helps greatly to develop a genial personality because, as Charles Schwab said, the man with it is bound to accomplish more than the man without it.
4. Many of the secrets in this book are subliminal. Read between the lines of the inspiring sales stories to see how you can apply the content to your own life.

CHAPTER 6

I CALL IT DYNAMIC PSYCHOLOGY

*"All cases are unique, and
very similar to others."*

T. S. ELIOT

In days gone by, in the not so dim and distant past, many people have tried to gain the secrets of success through means of the occult, astrology, tea leaves, palm readings and the tarot. However, profits, not prophets, foretell the future — and it is only in recent years that psychology has really taken a firm, large and powerful role in the accumulation of wealth.

Why is it that some people appear to have vibrant, dynamic personalities and can sell themselves and their wares to anyone, anyplace, night or day? Others, although they appear to try hard, remain ineffective. Why is it some people always say the right thing at precisely the right time and always say exactly what the prospect wants to hear, while others appear to be con men, or just plain insincere? Why is it some men are like King Midas, in that everything they touch turns to gold? Those men appear to be money magnets. Others, it would seem, repel wealth, although they may be trying hard to accumulate it. The answers are all in this book, and when you're wise to all this, you'll understand how to gain wealth instead of turning it away.

There is a classic story of a door-to-door salesman who, every time a little old lady dressed in her nightgown and slippers and with her hair in curlers opened the door, would say, "Hello, dear, is your mother in?" Some may call this flattery, others call it psychology. Whichever, it is salesmanship at its lowest possible ebb, and in any case I am not sure the story is true.

Dynamic psychology is as different from the above as chalk from cheese. It is of paramount importance that you remember it is not the specific example you must follow but the principle. In every case, it is the principle I am trying to hammer home.

Dynamic psychology is frighteningly powerful. In its various guises it can be used to ask an employer for a raise, persuade people to help you in your business career or lend you money. You can use dynamic psychology for making a date with someone or even persuading the person of your choice to marry you. It can also be used to inspire salesmen and motivate employees as well as to increase your sales. It can enable you to make deals and buy things at your price. You can use it successfully whether you are climbing the corporate, or the entrepreneurial ladder.

Every successful deal or transaction revolves around Dynamic Psychology. There is a definite pattern to a successful conclusion of any such deal and, although each case is unique in some respects, in certain fundamental ways it is similar to others.

Dynamic Psychology can be compared to a grappling hook. You have seen films of Marines throwing a grappling hook either up a cliff or onto the roof of a steep building they are about to climb. The grappling hook usually comes tumbling back down on the first and second throws. This is just to create drama and suspense in the film. But on the third throw the grappling hook is always securely lodged in place and the Marines scale their objective. When you use dynamic psychology it always works, without fail, it is just like a four-pronged grappling hook — it gets stuck in there!

To get down to the nitty-gritty of what makes a successful salesman we must break the whole concept of selling down to its nuts and bolts.

The first important point to recognize is that conning and selling are two different things, not one, as so many salesmen seem to think. Conning is when the transaction is based on the emotion of greed. If I were to sell the Eiffel Tower or set up any other con, I would get my "mark" to believe he was in on the ground floor of the operation. Then I would tell him that in order to conclude the deal before anybody else could upset things and escalate the price, he would have to keep absolutely quiet. His greed for the bait would keep him quiet and by the time he had discovered that I had conned him, I would have disappeared. The nuts and bolts of a con trick are simple: The con is based on greed, the "mark" doesn't get anything for his money and the seller disappears. One other thing about the con — your business is always diminishing because you can't con the same person twice.

Selling is totally different. Selling is based on the premise that the sale benefits the purchaser and the seller mutually. The purchaser may receive a car and the salesman may receive money. The mechanics of selling are simple: both buyer and seller get something from the transaction, both should be satisfied, both are still around after the transaction is concluded, both can talk openly about the transaction and the business should be always increasing because, unlike the con, you not only hope to sell to the prospect again, but to his children and even their children when the time comes.

If your sales presentation is full of holes or is wishy-washy and you have tried to talk your customer into something or out of something by lying and deceiving, you are no better than a con man. In most cases you will get a cancelled check, a cancelled sale or a loss of commission. Somewhere down the line you will lose.

The art of selling is not to persuade your prospect to just hand over a deposit and sign on the dotted line, but to have it be, in the *prospect's* best judgement, the product or service that best fills his needs. The prospect should leave convinced that he or she couldn't have got a better deal elsewhere. And when he or she is ready for another one of whatever it is you are selling he or she will come back to you for it. That's selling!

Fortunately for me, on most of the occasions when I have been called a good salesman, people were studying my sales figures and track record. But when a prospect to whom you are actually talking says, "You are a good salesman," you have failed. It simply means your art has been showing. Do not deliberately let any prospect know you are a salesman. The net is surely spread in vain when it can be seen by any bird! Never have dollar signs in your eyes, that's a dead giveaway. Sincerity is your highest priority.

It is at about this time that I suspect you want me to show you how to close deals, with, I suppose, stereotype closes. Many people have written books on how to close sales, and the damage they have done is immeasurable. Books on how to close deals breed stereotype salesmen who get the impression that there is one particular way to close any kind of deal. It's absurd to even imagine that a certain set of words will automatically close a deal. No two prospects think alike, act alike or want the same thing from a deal. I even know salesmen who spend a lot of time talking about closes that they have read about in books. Admittedly they make terrific stories, they are good entertainment, but you can't use them! I, personally, have closed literally thousands of deals, but I have never used a closing procedure I read about in a book. I could write a book on closes myself, but they wouldn't do *you* any good, because they are the closes *I* used to close certain deals, with certain people, on certain occasions. I've never used the same closing procedure more than once. I doubt I'll ever use the same ones again, simply because circumstances never exactly repeat themselves. The people who write about closing deals couldn't possibly have known for sure what words would be successful in closing a deal until they actually closed the deal.

Successful communication, persuasion and selling can't be done consciously — it is a product of the subconscious. If you converse consciously you disrupt the natural flow of communication. I don't know what I'm going to say to a certain prospect until I meet him. Many times I don't even know what I'm going to say until I hear myself actually saying it!

Unfortunately, all too often, even really good salesmen fall into the trap of writing books about selling. They observe what is currently available and write books in accordance with what is generally accepted. They write books on what they *think* they are doing. Unfortunately, writing about what they *think* they do isn't good enough, simply because all the important things they do are done subconsciously. Therefore, they themselves don't even realize what they are doing.

I have devoted a lot of time to the study of what I call dynamic psychology, or how to persuade men to buy things and do things, but at the same time make them think it was their own idea and decision.

Let us briefly examine the concept of what I call dynamic psychology. "Dynamic" means "of force producing motion, active, potent, energetic, forceful." Enough said! The word "psychology" is derived from two Greek words, "psyche," meaning "mind or soul," and "logos," meaning study. Hence psychology means the study of the mind. The objective of dynamic psychology is to enable you to understand, predict and, if necessary, control and manipulate human behaviour to enable you to sell, motivate, progress and accumulate.

The only word emphasized here is the word study. Dynamic psychology is the result of a great deal of study of the best professional communicators in the world. I've done this both in person and from many hours of listening to and watching video recordings. The important thing about dynamic psychology is that it isn't what these super super salesmen think they are doing when they sell successfully. It isn't what I think they are doing when they are persuading somebody to buy something. Dynamic psychology is what they actually do, whether they realize it or not, when they are selling successfully.

What I will give you are the components of Dynamic Psychology. These components are not presented in any particular order, firstly, because you can't use any one on its own, and, secondly, because they are to be combined with a secret we mentioned earlier. The secret is selling in a conversational manner and selling a good product or service. Finally, some of the things I will show you initially are to form a groundwork for other things you are required to do throughout your sales presentation.

SELL TO YOUR PROSPECTS' SYSTEM

In the chapter on goals we saw how we use our internal processing in three ways: we see pictures in our minds (visual), we talk within ourselves and hear voices within (auditory) and we feel and have emotions (kinesthetic). We saw that although we each use the three processes, each of us uses one more than the other two. Selling is simply a matter of effective and persuasive communication. The more persuasive you are and the better you communicate, the more you sell.

One demonstration I particularly like to perform when I have a large audience is to carefully explain the three processing systems. I then ask the members of the audience which of them spend most of their processing time visualizing. Up go a crop of hands. I then ask those who spend most of their processing time feeling a lot and having emotions to raise their hands. Finally, I ask the members of the audience who think out verbally and listen to internal voices to raise their hands. I then ask how many of them are amazed that so many of the other people don't do their thinking and processing the same way that they do. *All* the hands go up. *All* the members of the audience are amazed that everyone else doesn't think and process in the same way they themselves do.

One of the first things you must do is call your "Think Tank" together. This is the group of six or eight people for whom you will buy a copy of this book. These are the people who will help you build your fortune. Have a discussion about how each does his processing. Label yourselves kinesthetic, visual or auditory in accordance with how you spend the greater part of your processing time.

An easy way to establish what you and your associates are is to imagine someone has just put a deal or proposition to you. Those who go inside and process the deal with feeling and emotions will want the deal to have the right "feel" about it. They will say something on the order of "Yes, it's a good deal, it feels right, " or "I can't get a handle on it." These are kinesthetic people. Those who go inside and process the deal internally by talking it out and listening to voices in their heads will say, "Yes, that sounds like a good deal to me," or "I don't like the tone of it." These people are certainly auditory. Finally those who process visually will look at their mental pictures and, if they like what they see, they will say. "What a bright idea," or "It looks good to me." These people are visuals.

Once you grasp the fact that people think and process in three totally different ways, you immediately become aware of why it is some strangers you meet are immediately on your wavelength and why you can't communicate with others, no matter how hard you try.

What happens is this: perhaps you are kinesthetic and the stranger you bump into or try to sell to is also kinesthetic. You can then immediately relate to one another, because you both process by feeling. Even if you don't feel identical things, you can feel for one another and experience situations in the same way.

Let's look at another situation. Let's assume you are kinesthetic, but the person that you are trying to sell is visual. While you are talking to him in your feeling and emotional way, he may not be able to relate to you, because he is expending energy in the attempt to translate feelings into pictures. However, the emotions and feelings you have don't readily convert into pictures. The pictures he comes up with in his mind's eye might bear no resemblance to the way you understand the deal. You're each in entirely different modes.

Another illustration: let's assume you are visual. The person you are trying to sell is auditory. What you may tell that prospect may be absolutely clear and convincing to you because you can see it clearly in the form of a picture in your mind's eye. But the auditory person will proceed to discuss verbally within himself whatever deal or proposition you have put to him. He will talk it out as logically as he can in his mind. He will spend time trying to convert your picture to words. Even if you have carefully conveyed every bit of the picture that was in your mind's eye, what you say may still not make sense to him. He or she will assume you are talking illogically!

The problem may sound complex, but the solution is a simple one. Carefully analyse how you yourself deal with your internal processing. Do you feel a great deal and have a lot of emotions? Do you talk out situations and listen to voices in your head? Or do you spend most of your time dealing with pictures in your mind's eye? Don't forget we all use *all* of the systems, but each of us uses *one* more than the others. The one we use the most is what makes us either visual, kinesthetic or auditory.

When you have decided what category you belong to keep it in mind. When you have a prospect in front of you convey everything you have within you to him in all three systems. Talk logically and let him hear the appropriate sounds, get through to his feelings and emotions and use visual aids to enable him to see what it is you are talking about. While you are talking to your prospect you must get into the habit of going inside yourself and saying "How does it feel, look and sound to him?" Whether you realize it or not, all the time you are talking, your prospect is either visualizing, or paying attention to his feelings, or talking to himself.

To become a successful salesman you must assume that the person standing in front of you may be using a different processing system than yourself. To be able to sell to him or her you have to talk his or her system, at least part of the time. People give subconscious clues all the time about what system they use. One may say, "well it looks to me," or "the way I see it." This person is visual. Another may say "I said to myself," or "it sounds like." This person is auditory. Or perhaps you have heard others say, "I feel as though," or "It just feels right." These people are kinesthetic. You can and must pick up these clues. The clues will allow you to communicate better with your prospect. If you can determine what process your prospect uses, you can package your sales pitch in such a way that it will be totally irresistible for him or her.

Imagine you are selling a car. It is easy to see that a Visual will want the car to *look* right, have the right lines, and the right colour. The auditory will not only make sure the engine *sounds* right, but he will also make sure the radio sounds good, the doors don't clunk, and the windows don't squeak when rolled up.

85

The Kinesthetic will definitely want to drive the car to make sure it *feels* right and to make sure the seats are comfortable and the steering is light and positive.

Now, this is the important point: because we all use all of the processing systems, each of those three prospects will be interested in all of the above mentioned items, but each will be more interested in *one* aspect than in the other two. It would be no good at all if you were trying to sell a car on its appearance when what the prospect really wanted to know was how the car felt.

You must pick up on the subconscious verbal and non-verbal signals your prospect puts out. If he responds favourably to what you say about the car's looks and colour, you can assume he's a Visual and proceed to concentrate on visual aspects such as the walnut dashboard, the magnesium wheels, the metallic paint and the red-leather interior. You must determine whether your prospect is a Visual, an Auditory or a Kinesthetic and, bearing in mind what process he uses, proceed to sell him.

If you are trying to sell him one way and he's not responding favourably it is *you* who are doing something wrong and *you* who must try something else. If a prospect asks you about specific features of a car, categorize those features as visual, auditory or kinesthetic and commence to sell him on those terms. If you don't know the processing system he's using, guess. Direct your sales pitch toward one system, and see what response you get. Alter your behaviour accordingly.

All too often salesmen ramble on and on, without bothering to pick up their prospect's subconscious signals. They do not keep altering their sales pitch until the prospect shows enthusiasm. Then they wonder why they don't make sales. They give exactly the same spiel no matter who the person is, how he thinks or what he actually wants.

It doesn't make an iota of difference whether you are selling cars or the Amway plan, cosmetics or real estate, it matters not whether you sell tangibles or intangibles — persuasion and communication is the name of the game.

When you sell you must talk with feeling and emotion. At the same time, tug at heartstrings and talk with humour. That will appeal to the Kinesthetic. For appeal to the Visual, you must point out all the visual aspects of what you are selling, and you must paint glossy pictures with words to enable your prospect to visualize in his or her mind's eye. Furthermore, for appeal to the Auditory, you must talk logically and let the customer hear relevant sounds and noises. You must sell like this to communicate with all three of the processing systems.

It is for these reasons that any successful politician, public speaker or businessman addressing a crowd of people will talk the way he does. Although he will talk as if in a one-to-one situation, he will tug at heartstrings, reduce people to tears, mix his speech with humour and talk logically and rationally. He gets through to emotions as well as to reason, and he also uses appropriate illustrations. Because it's the only way you can sell to the three systems at the same time, this is the only way you can get a favorable response from a crowd of people.

If you want further examples on how to sell, just read this book a few times. You will see that it is written exactly the way I sell. I paint glossy pictures, I tell stories with emotion and feeling. At the same time I tug at the heartstrings and, mixing it with humour, I put over what I have to say logically. It doesn't matter whether a Kinesthetic, a Visual or an Auditory is reading the book, each one can relate to it! That's how you must sell! The more you can grasp and absorb about people using different processing systems, the easier you will find it to sell to anyone you come across; know-it-alls included.

By studying people you will soon see that auditory people make great telephone salespeople because all they need is a voice to be able to relate to someone. Visuals make terrible telephone salespeople because they need eye-to-eye contact.

Typically, visual people complain that Auditories, because they often don't make eye contact during conversation, aren't paying attention to them. Likewise, Kinesthetics complain that Visual and Auditory people are often insensitive. Auditory people are always complaining that Kinesthetic people don't listen. If you have difficulty understanding or communicating with someone, it's almost bound to be because he or she uses a different processing system than yours.

Visuals make fast readers because all they have to do is look at the words to understand them. Meanwhile, Auditories make slow readers, because invariably they will be pronouncing and saying each word internally.

Visuals make great salesmen for selling tangible items such as jewelry, art, cars, clothing and, in fact, anything that has to look good. The Auditory best sells intangibles such as consultancy or insurance and is also good at telephone sales or selling musical goods and instruments. The Kinesthetic can sell anything that has to do with feel or touch. That includes silks, furs, sports equipment that has to feel right, real estate that has to feel like a home or travel tours that have to feel right. Also, they make good funeral directors, therapists and psychiatrists because they are good at dealing with people's emotions.

Henry Ford once pointed out that "If there is any one secret of success, it lies in the ability to get the other person's point of view and see things from his own angle as well as from your own." Ford knew how to do this intuitively. Unfortunately he never divulged exactly how the layman could do it. It is simple enough: to be a good salesman who can sell anything is simply a matter of developing one's own processing systems and recognizing the processing system of the person you are selling. By presenting your sales pitch in a way that is consistent with your prospect's processing system, you make your ideas and goods maximally acceptable to him. By matching your words and strategy to his processing system, you exert a powerful influence on his purchasing decision. The psychological tools outlined in this chapter are phenomenally powerful because they affect a person below his or her threshold of consciousness.

Another system I want to just briefly mention, without going into it too deeply, is the olfactory system. "Olfactory" refers to our processing of taste and smell. It is a system all of us use, but only to a very small degree. In contrast, the olfactory system in animals is usually the most highly developed. It is used for finding food, for smelling out enemies and for finding a mate. In humans, the olfactory is not well developed. It hasn't always been like that, early Red Indians used to be able to smell a white man or a buffalo from fifteen to twenty miles away. However today, the mere struggle for food and survival in the Western world is no longer top priority. Therefore our olfactory ability is diminishing. However, it is still there, in each and every one of us, and the star salesman is the first to recognize it and use it in his sales presentation. For instance, a new car has a smell of its own. The first thing I used to do when selling new cars was to get my prospect in the car so he could get a whiff of that new interior. When selling genuine leather coats or belts, let your customer smell the genuine leather, appeal to his or her olfactory system. When I was selling property, I used to air empty houses out so that they smelled fresh, not stale and musty. I would point this out in a subtle way to my prospects. Whenever you can get to a person's olfactory system, do so — it is still there and it is still powerful. Making use of this system adds one more tool to your psychological tool box!

To become a good salesman, direct your sales pitch to all three processing systems. To become a super, super salesman, direct most of your sales pitch to the system your prospect *uses the most*. In either case, it will help you tremendously if you cultivate the two systems you use least. Then you can really understand how other people do their processing. You can do this simply. If you are an auditory, you must practice visualizing things in your mind's eye and creating mental images. Also, you must develop your emotions and feelings. Become more sensitive to situations and people. It will also help if you develop your tactile sense. It is another area in which kinesthetics are developed. If you are a visual, you must practise talking out deals within yourself and, also, develop your kinesthetic processing system. If you are a Kinesthetic, you must practice making pictures in your mind's eye and talking within yourself. Work hard at developing the systems you use least and you will be able to sell to anybody!

SUBCONSCIOUS RAPPORT

Before we go any further into the components of dynamic psychology I want to make an important suggestion. This suggestion is so important that I would say if you were going to get one thing only out of this book, let it be this one thing: the vast subconscious mind is literally the foundation of everything we do.

You have had a lot of proof that the subconscious is the largest part of the mind. We have already used it for visualizing, for providing Eurekas! and for problem solving. When we sell, we must direct most of our efforts towards penetrating the subconscious minds of our prospects. We must get below their threshold of consciousness.

One of the most important things we must do is establish subconscious rapport with our prospects.

This is the great secret I was talking about earlier that is used by all super, super salesmen who don't even realize they are doing it. If there is a common denominator in the breed of super, super salesmen, it is, paradoxically, that they are all different. Different, that is, in every respect except one: without fail they all establish subconscious rapport before they try to sell a prospect.

The best way to establish subconscious rapport is to very subtly follow your prospect's subconscious habits. You must do this on both a verbal and non-verbal basis. If he or she breathes lightly, pick up his exact way and rhythm of breathing. If he or she happens to be asthmatic, breathe deeply and heavily, just the same as the prospect does. The prospect probably drinks his or her coffee in a certain way. Copy this as closely as you can. He is bound to blink his eyelids either quickly or slowly and he might become flustered. Whatever he does subconsciously make sure your movements pick up on his and subtly mimic them. The super, super salesmen do this and don't even realize they do it!

On many occasions I have told these super, super salesmen just what it is that they do. Only after showing them several examples of their subconscious behavior do they believe me. One salesman used to carry most of the popular brands of cigarettes with him. When his prospect lit up a certain brand, this salesman made sure he pulled out the same kind of cigarette. He thought it was "nice" if he could offer the prospect the same brand of cigarette that he smoked normally. But what this salesman was *really* doing was establishing subconscious rapport, and he didn't even realize it!

If your prospect runs his fingers through his hair, you, a little later, should do the same. Make sure you are not obvious about what you are doing. Don't forget you are only trying to get through to your prospect's *subconscious*. You certainly don't want him to notice *consciously*. Your prospect may take his glasses and wipe them in a certain manner. Copy that manner exactly. The nearer you copy his subconscious activities, both verbal and non-verbal, the sooner you are going to establish subconscious rapport — and be on the same wavelength.

Perhaps you're dealing with someone who is hard-boiled and spits on the ground occasionally. Well, that's a subconscious habit and the sooner you mimic it, the sooner you are going to be taking money off the man.

If you're having lunch with a prospect and he orders a cold salad and a glass of orange juice, your order of hot stew and a glass of wine immediately alienates him. Not only would I order exactly the same thing as my prospect, but I would mimic his eating patterns and habits. I would pace my eating to that of my prospect, and I would finish my meal when he finishes his. I would let his subconscious know we were on the same wavelength.

If a prospect offers me a cup of coffee, I will accept. I automatically assume that this person has a cup of coffee at three o'clock every afternoon. It's a subconscious habit and I'll follow it to the letter. To do so establishes subconscious rapport. Not to do so alienates me from the prospect subconsciously. You can do the same. Subconscious rapport is the thing that makes friends automatically!

Success in large measures is due to powerful subconscious rapport with prospects more than it is to all other factors, and methods, involved in selling. People must be able to relate to you. Most of this rapport is on a subconscious level.

You must get below the threshold of consciousness. The ways to do that have been presented here. The successful salesman must learn many different types of behaviour in the same way, really, that an actor does, so that many different personalities can relate to him.

The more types of behaviour he can cultivate and carry off, the more people will relate to him, and the more successful he will be. Copy that facial expression, copy the way your prospect holds his martini and the way he leans on the bar. Mimic it exactly. Let that man's subconscious know that you are both on the same wavelength. If your prospect clasps his hands, twitches his top lip or mops his brow, copy his behaviour to the letter.

The prospect's subconscious is able to relate to yours and in actual fact what it sees is a mirror image of itself — that can't be bad. In effect what his subconscious is saying, "when you put your sales story over like that, how can I possibly argue with *myself!*"

By speaking and behaving in the same way as your prospect, you give the prospect a sense that his inner world is understood. Although your behaviour won't be recognized consciously, your words and actions have a profound effect on the prospect's subconscious. However, if your actions are noticed consciously, you are overacting. Be subtle.

My behaviour pattern alters dramatically, depending on whom I'm selling to. For selling motorcycles to Hells Angels, I wore denims and long hair and acted like they did. When I was a business consultant to a multi-million dollar corporation, I wore short hair and sported three-piece suits, and was, to all intents and purposes, a whiz kid. And for selling home appliances to housewives it was slacks, sweaters and sports jackets — a charming, casual approach.

An indication of the effectiveness of this was that each of these completely diverse groups said of me, "He's one of us!" I hope this brings home to you how much I am prepared to alter my behaviour. I alter it still further when dealing with separate individuals. On many occasions I have been called a "Master of the Art of Persuasion." I should, really, be called "Master of the Art of Establishing Subconscious Rapport"

— because without the rapport there is no persuasion and without the persuasion there are no sales.

You must also establish subconscious rapport by copying your prospect's speech patterns, tone, tempo and sentence structure. Perhaps your prospect talks with a plum in his mouth, you must mirror this and do the same. Or, if he talks like a roughneck, or swears, mimic that behaviour as well. Tonality also counts for a great deal, and never get away from the fact it is futile to try and sell something before you have established subconscious rapport.

Perhaps the most important thing of all is using the same sentence structure your prospect does. When I say "sentence structure," I simply mean using the same types of words that your prospect uses to describe things. He will either use auditory, kinesthetic or visual words to describe his experiences and feelings. For example, as a business consultant suppose I have a client in front of me who says "Do you see what I mean" or "I'm trying to give you a clear perspective of. . ." My reply is: "I get the picture." The client is talking like a Visual, so I reply using the same subconscious language.

Another client says to me "I feel as though. . ." or "It's particularly hard when you're up against a solid brick wall." So I reply, "Yes, I'm sure we can smooth things out by carefully handling the creditors and. . ." My client is using feeling words, so I reply kinesthetically.

The third client says "I know it sounds like I'm whining, but when these creditors shout at me and crack the whip it really makes me scream." So I talk auditorily to him. I say "We can simply tune in with your creditors by meeting them and harmonizing the whole situation — then they won't have anything to screech at."

Never lose sight of the fact that although your prospect might not appreciate consciously that you are using the same sentence structure, it will have a profound effect on his subconscious. In every case I pick up on the client's voice, tone, pattern and tempo as well as using the same sentence structure he does.

The amateur salesman sounds as though he is trying to purposely alienate himself. Here is a typical exchange. The prospect says, "Yes, the problem looks as though you could see through it, but I'm still very vague on the details and can't seem to focus on the..." The amateur replies, "Yeah, it sounds as though. . ." He is using auditory words and begins his sentence with "Yeah," while his prospect is using visual works and says "Yes." He'll never sell that prospect anything.

The easiest way to establish subconscious rapport is to enter your prospect's inner reality. By becoming part of it, you join his inner world. By speaking in the same way your prospect does and using the same sentence structure that he does, you automatically build up subconscious trust. That trust is extremely important if you are trying to relieve a prospect of his or her money.

One particular guy who owned a lot of desirable property was causing my associates anguish because they couldn't deal with him. In fact he wouldn't deal with them. The property was needed to enable us to have a complete land tract with no third parties on it. I got an introduction to the property owner and went around to see him. It seems funny now, but this guy was watching television. I sat down and watched with him. I adopted the same body posture and breathing rate as my prospect. When the program finished he switched off the television and we started talking. Initially we started talking about the guy who gave me the introduction. I noticed that my prospect talked very slowly, so that's how I talked *to him*, while retaining his body posture and breathing rate. After about an hour, he suddenly asked me if I felt like going to the bar down the street for a drink. No sooner were we in the bar than my prospect's speech pattern changed dramatically. He began to talk very quickly. He talked about everything and anything. And I mean everything! I altered the speed of my conversation to match his and talked about the same things he talked about. Most important of all, I noticed that my prospect used many words like "pushy", "feel", "cold", "comfort", "grasp" and "contact". These are all kinesthetic words, so in my conversation I purposely used words like "tight", "handle", "warmth", "rough" and "soft" — also kinesthetic words. When we left the bar and returned to my prospect's house, he again relapsed into very slow speech patterns and I followed suit. I left him that evening on a happy note and told him I'd drop over again. I hadn't mentioned business all evening. Why? What would be the point? I had spent the evening establishing subconscious rapport.

A few evenings later I went around again and followed practically the same routine, talking slowly to begin with. When he asked once more if I wanted to go to the bar, I accepted. At the bar the tempo went up and on return it dropped back down again. I was, again, careful to adopt his body posture, hand movements, breathing rate, speech patterns and sentence structure.

This happened five or six times. Then one evening, when I was at the prospect's house, I asked him if he wanted to go for a drink. He accepted, and that was the beginning of the rapport that I had been establishing. For a while I let the asking alternate, and eventually I suggested we go to a different bar. When my prospect would follow *my* suggestions and behaviour, I knew subconscious rapport had been established. Now I could deal with him on my terms. Which I did — successfully. I can only describe this prospect's behaviour as schizophrenic, in that he would adopt one personality one hour and a different one the next. There is no limit to the variety of human behaviour. The only thing various behaviours have in common is that they can be paced and mirrored. You may never have to alternate behaviour depending on location as I did, but if the occasion presents itself you should be prepared.

You must be flexible in your behaviour and the way you present yourself until you get the rapport and response you want. More than any other factor involved in selling, you should work *hard* on being like the prospect. Let his inner world know that the two of you are on the same wavelength.

There was yet another prospect none of my associates could deal with. This particular prospect was what I call the nervous, flustered type. Within the first hour of our meeting, he dropped his cigarette on the floor three times. I don't smoke, so I emulated his behaviour by dropping my pencil on the floor three times in the exact manner he dropped his cigarette. I noticed he breathed very heavily and sat tensed in his chair. I copied his behaviour to the letter. Also, when explaining, he would gesticulate in a flustered way and his words were frequently jumbled. I copied the exact flustered movement of his hands and I jumbled my words in the same way. This guy used many auditory words in his sentence structure, and I made sure that I did also. His favorite sayings were "That rings a bell," "I can resonate with that," and "I hear you, man." He also used many words like "scream", "shout", "harmonize" and "tone". So I used as many auditory words as I could. I used "loud", "amplify", "tune", "hear" and "listen". I managed to sell to this guy on our first meeting.

Remember one thing, there is no such thing as a resistant prospect. It is *you* who resists becoming like that prospect. He will never become like you or understand you. You must convince him or her that you have kindred interests and the way to do that is to convince the prospect you are kindred spirits. Establish

97

subconscious rapport, then sell the product.

There was a third individual I was trying to motivate into increasing sales in one of my shops. I noticed that every time I was with him he would blow hard three times out his nose every ten or fifteen minutes. So, I mirrored that, but I was careful not to be as audible as he was. This was just one of this guy's particular quirks that I mirrored. Actually, I mirrored and paced a total of about six specific things he did. He also used words like "focus", "clear", "bright" and "red" as well as saying "I see what you mean" and "It looks to me," which are all visual words or phrases. Typically, I used the same sentence structure as he did, and included words like "see", "vague", "picture", "flash" and "blue" — all visual words. I managed to motivate this guy to his fullest potential simply by getting on his wavelength before I gradually got him onto my wavelength.

Realize that practically everything you do has an effect on your prospect's subconscious mind. These things will either alienate you from, or ally you to, the person you are dealing with. To establish subconscious rapport, *you* must become like *him*.

The subconscious mind, like the part of an iceberg under water, is eight times as large and infinitely more powerful than the top part, or the conscious mind. Recognize your power as an individual, the power of the subconscious, and stop acting like those who have never even thought about it. Everything you do on a conscious level when you try to sell a prospect has little or no effect compared with the vast influence you have on someone subconsciously. Subconscious rapport is the thing that makes great salesmen and allows you to communicate with anybody.

SUBCONSCIOUS MESSAGES AND SIGNALS

When a prospect says to me that he's "not sure," or "no," or he behaves negatively, I never believe him. What I do believe, however, are his subconscious signals. Let me illustrate: when you were a child and had done something slightly dangerous, your father may have told you off, but at the same time he smiled and patted you on the back. At another time, when things in the family seemed uncertain, your mother told you that everything was okay, but her teeth were gritted, her hands were cold and her eyes watered. Perhaps someone told you that they loved you, but they never spoke warmly, gave praise or showed support. In all these cases you don't really believe what you are being told. You believe the subconscious message.

It doesn't matter what people tell you, it is the subconscious signals you must read. If you receive negative subconscious signals from your prospect, you must alter your way of selling to that prospect until you achieve the desired response. All along, watch and listen carefully to see if what you are saying is appealing to your prospect.

One of the most powerful subconscious signals you can pick up comes from the eyes. A person's eyes speak a whole subconscious language of their own. Rudolf Valentino, during his whole film career, never spoke a word, but his eyes sold him to millions, particularly to women. Those eyes were full of love and romance. Charlie Chaplin was another actor whose eyes could express a wide range of feeling: humour, love, sadness, stupidity or whatever other emotion he was conveying. You must be familiar with the signals a girl across the room at a party is giving. Her eyes will tell you everything you want to know! You must also recognize the looks your wife or girlfriend gives you when she sees you looking back over your shoulder at that same girl. You have heard the expression, "If looks could kill," or "She gave me the glad eye," or "He's down in the dumps — look at his sad eyes." Also, "She's got an eye for you," "He had a twinkle in his eye," and "He wouldn't want to fight me because he knows I'd beat him; he can tell just by looking in my eyes."

Through their subconscious language people literally tell you what processing system they are using. Generally speaking, a person's eyes look up when he is visualizing; they go down and to the left if someone is talking internally; and down and to the right if someone is feeling emotions. This information is valuable to the salesman simply because it helps him read his prospect's mind quickly and better. If the prospect's eyes keep going up, he's obviously processing by visualizing, so you will want to sell him on a visual level. You will point out visual aspects, paint pictures for your prospect and use visual aids. Perhaps his eyes keep going down and to the right. You will want to sell to him kinesthetically and get into his emotions. Once you have established which processing system the prospect uses the most, you can really sell on a level that will appeal to him.

You can check the validity of what I say about eye movements by calling your "Think Tank" — your close advisors — together and asking them to imagine various things. You don't want them to answer you verbally — just get them to internally process the information. For example, get them to process visual information. Tell them to imagine what their mothers look like; tell them to try to recall what color is on the top of the traffic lights; or tell them to visualize what an elephant looks like. If you watch the eyes of the people you question you will notice that to process visual information their eyes look up.

Now ask them to process some auditory information: Imagine what a racing car sounds like; imagine how a dripping faucet sounds; or the noise a jet makes taking off. Watch their eyes go down and to the left.

Now try kinesthetic statements: What does sandpaper feel like? How do you feel when you are angry?

just wake up? When people
rmation — any information
feeling, or emotions — their
e right as they process the

sales presentation you should
ect's eyes go most often dur-
then see what processing
your sales pitch according to
nd equally as important, as
direction you can assume he
to process. It is at this very
p talking, even if only briefly,
to have time to process. To
the amateur salesman, only
ospect. Everyone needs time
nted to him. So stop reading
e information I just told you.
right?

do is actually indicate, phy-
nternal processing they are
meone processing kinesthet-
, rub his thigh, or caress his
telling you he is *feeling* his
funny habit of holding on to
s. Subconsciously he's telling
y and listening to voices in
tly rubs his eyes as if to say
h, of course, he is.

esman you must make use of
gnals. Some salesmen totally
signals, yet you know, and
be saying the exact opposite
eling and thinking. The only
d upon are the things your
sciously.

shrewd old businessmen who
even catatonic, with poker

101

playing faces, in an endeavour to try not to give out subconscious signals. Little do they realize human beings can't "not-communicate." Whatever feedback you are getting is the communication. When you learn how to read people, that's all you need. In any case these people who think they are offering no communication have eyes moving about in their heads telling you what processing system they are using, and that's exactly what you want to know.

When a boy says to a girl that he loves her, she will, if she's got any sense, pay more attention to the tone of his voice and his subconscious signals than to the actual words. So many salesmen attract negative results solely by using the wrong tone of voice. They say all the right words but in the wrong tone — consequently they never sell. You can get different responses from people simply by altering just your tone of voice.

You must learn what people really mean and want, and the only way to do it is to recognize subconscious signals. If you are getting negative subconscious signals, alter your behaviour until you get the desired results. There is no need to take "no" for an answer, because you are in complete control. It helps tremendously if you realize people's internal organization is extremely chaotic. It's frightening to think that because of this you can sell most people simply by understanding them and selling to their processing system in a way that makes absolutely perfect sense to them. Furthermore, and I'll say it again, if what you are doing and saying isn't getting through and producing desired results *you* must alter *your* behaviour until it does.

Make sure you never yawn in front of a prospect. Be absolutely aware of your own subconscious behaviour. Realize that even if your prospect doesn't notice any of your negative and unfavourable behaviour consciously, he certainly will subconsciously.

The successful salesman must know what outcome he wants from each deal. Also, he must have a wide

How do you feel when you just wake up? When people process kinesthetic information — any information that has to do with touch, feeling, or emotions — their eyes go down and to the right as they process the information.

In the course of your sales presentation you should observe where your prospect's eyes go most often during processing. You can then see what processing system he uses and direct your sales pitch according to that system. Secondly, and equally as important, as his eyes move in any one direction you can assume he has gone inside himself to process. It is at this very moment that you must stop talking, even if only briefly, to enable your prospect to have time to process. To ramble on and on, like the amateur salesman, only serves to confuse the prospect. Everyone needs time to process material presented to him. So stop reading for a moment, process the information I just told you. Does it look, sound or feel right?

Another thing people do is actually indicate, physically, the system of internal processing they are using. For example, someone processing kinesthetically will stroke his chin, rub his thigh, or caress his arms. He will literally be telling you he is *feeling* his way. The Auditory has a funny habit of holding on to his ear or touching his lips. Subconsciously he's telling you he's talking internally and listening to voices in his head. The Visual gently rubs his eyes as if to say he's a seeing person, which, of course, he is.

To become a star salesman you must make use of all these subconscious signals. Some salesmen totally disregard subconscious signals, yet you know, and they know, that you can be saying the exact opposite of what you are really feeling and thinking. The only things that can be relied upon are the things your prospect tells you subconsciously.

I have met so-called shrewd old businessmen who remain expressionless, even catatonic, with poker playing faces, in an endeavour to try not to give out subconscious signals. Little do they realize human beings can't "not-communicate." Whatever feedback you are getting is the communication. When you learn how to read people, that's all you need. In any case these people who think they are offering no communication have eyes moving about in their heads telling you what processing system they are using, and that's exactly what you want to know.

When a boy says to a girl that he loves her, she will, if she's got any sense, pay more attention to the tone of his voice and his subconscious signals than to the actual words. So many salesmen attract negative results solely by using the wrong tone of voice. They say all the right words but in the wrong tone — consequently they never sell. You can get different responses from people simply by altering just your tone of voice.

You must learn what people really mean and want, and the only way to do it is to recognize subconscious signals. If you are getting negative subconscious signals, alter your behaviour until you get the desired results. There is no need to take "no" for an answer, because you are in complete control. It helps tremendously if you realize people's internal organization is extremely chaotic. It's frightening to think that because of this you can sell most people simply by understanding them and selling to their processing system in a way that makes absolutely perfect sense to them. Furthermore, and I'll say it again, if what you are doing and saying isn't getting through and producing desired results *you* must alter *your* behaviour until it does.

Make sure you never yawn in front of a prospect. Be absolutely aware of your own subconscious behaviour. Realize that even if your prospect doesn't notice any of your negative and unfavourable behaviour consciously, he certainly will subconsciously.

The successful salesman must know what outcome he wants from each deal. Also, he must have a wide range of behaviours and use those behaviours appropriately to establish subconscious rapport. He must also be flexible enough to alter his behaviour to achieve the required responses and he must also be sensitive enough to pick up subconscious signals.

Although there is a superabundance of knowledge about how to sell in just this one chapter, your real knowledge comes from discussing these techniques with members of your "Think Tank." When you actually see the eye movements and subconscious signals that I'm talking about, you'll soon become proficient in using these psychological tools.

When you come across someone whose eyes don't follow the patterns that I have described, don't panic. If you observe carefully, you will notice that that person always follows his own particular pattern; i.e., if he looks up to process kinesthetic questions and down and to the left to process visual questions, then that is the pattern he will always follow.

Have fun with your "Think Tank" discussing these subconscious signals and processing systems. Learn as much about them as you can before you actually put your knowledge into use. Believe me, there are definite reasons for being able to sell anyone anything and these reasons are outlined in this extremely powerful chapter. The object of dynamic psychology is to enable you to use the proper techniques knowingly. Only with practice will you succeed. The ultimate success for any professional persuader is to persuade subconsciously. The secret of success is not letting your prospect know you are mirroring his behaviour, picking up his subconscious signals, establishing rapport or selling to his processing system.

When you are selling, it is imperative that both your verbal and non-verbal subconscious messages match the words you are using to sell your prospect. Let me illustrate: Eddie was promoting the Amway plan. He told his prospects that he was excited and enthusiastic about it. However, he never laughed or even smiled. There were no excited gestures; he didn't act enthusiastic. Consequently, he never sponsored anybody. His prospects read the subconscious signals that said he was depressed and not doing well at all.

Kathy was a stockbroker. She advised her clients concerning their best interests, but they never followed through with what she advised. Although her words were the right ones, her subconscious signals told her clients that she was not at all confident. They acted on her subconscious signals, as people always do.

Melvin was an estate agent. Try hard as he would, he couldn't get enough listings or sell enough houses. Only when I met him did I realize that his subconscious signals told everybody that he thought the houses were priced too high and in terrible condition. Just his tone of voice, a dull monotone, was enough to put people off.

There are a few things you must do. First, recognize your own subconscious signals. Second, alter those signals until they match your words. You must observe these subconscious signals in your prospect too, for they are the only thing you can really rely on. Watch your prospect's verbal and non-verbal subconscious signals, because no matter what he tells you, the only part you can believe is what he tells you subconsciously. Furthermore, if his signals are negative, by altering your behaviour, tone, tempo, and sentence structure you can elicit a desirable response.

Say a man walks into your place of business and you ask if you can help him. He replies that he is just looking, and you immediately assume he is not interested. But this is a mistake, the mere fact that he is in your place of business is a subconscious signal that he's ready to buy, although he may not know it himself. Assume you are showing someone the Amway plan. The person says he is not interested, but does ask the occasional question about it. Subconsciously there is interest, whether it is realized or not. You must recognize these subconscious signals and act on them. Perhaps you are selling a man home insurance, and he says he's not interested. But somehow in his conversation a recent burglary at a neighbour's crops up. Well, let me tell you, that man is a hair's breadth away from buying, and he doesn't know it himself!

GATHERING INFORMATION IN ORDER TO SELL

The salesman who says that he can sell anything to anybody is a fool. He hasn't even started his apprenticeship. How can you sell a house with two bedrooms to a man with six children, a 60-foot yacht to a schoolboy who has only $40 or a size 10 dress to a size 18 woman? How can you borrow money from a man who hasn't got it? How can you ask someone for a raise if he doesn't have sufficient authority to give you one?

The star salesman makes a lot of sales, but very early on in his rapport with his prospect, he establishes in his mind whether or not it is conceivable that the two of them can do business, either immediately, sometime in the future or not at all. Once you have qualified whether your prospect is in a position to buy, you can go further into the selling process.

All too often the Apprentice Millionaire tries to sell before he has found out exactly what his prospect requires. By talking, asking questions and listening I can get the prospect to sell himself. The prospect simply tells me exactly what he or she requires and in doing so has made it possible for me to sell exactly what the prospect wants for the reasons he or she wants it.

By carefully drawing people out and listening to them, I can gather sufficient information to enable me to tell people exactly what they want to hear. I take particular note of the person's processing system and subconscious behaviour while at the same time I establish rapport. I can't possibly hope to sell anybody anything until I have established subconscious rapport, discovered his processing system and gathered enough information to enable me to tell him exactly what he wants to hear and needs to know.

A good analogy would be comparing a sale with a torpedo. The thousands of gallons of fuel and the engine of the torpedo are by far the largest part. They are not the reasons for the torpedo's existence, but they are all vital in getting the small warhead to its target. The warhead can be thought of as the actual sale. The huge amount of motor and fuel can be compared with the conversation and subliminal chatter that goes on before the sale. You can't have one without the other. Now you see why it is imperative to sell in a conversational manner. Only when I have done all this can I package the information about any service or product to *match* all the reasons that my prospect has given me both consciously and subconsciously for wanting to buy the product.

As a business consultant it is not unusual for me to spend five straight hours with a client. The first four hours I spend just asking questions and gathering information. How on earth can I proceed to help him sort out his business until I have found out everything about it? I spend the fifth hour telling my client what can be done and what to do, but not until I've gathered the information I need. By the time I have finished talking, asking questions and listening, my client has, himself, told me what is wrong and what needs to be done to put his business right. As a professional communicator, all I really do is to clearly relay back to him what needs to be done.

Far too many amateurs waste time talking about themselves. I can't see any benefit in that at all, but it *is* highly beneficial to have as much information about your prospect and his needs as is possible. I'm more interested in drawing my prospect out and listening to him than in anything else. This is the one way I can guarantee that everything I say will appeal to him. I can only manipulate and persuade people if I have some feedback from the person I'm trying to sell.

Many times in conversation I have a shortfall of knowledge or a shortfall of the true reasons why a prospect is not buying from me. I gather this knowledge by saying one simple word: "But?" For instance, a man may be interested in a car but is still not buying. I get him talking and he says it is just the colour, year and model that he wants. However, he's not buying. So I look him straight in the eye and, with his own tone of voice and say "But?" He automatically carries on: "*But* it's too expensive." I now have the vital missing information I need in order to keep on selling. I can justify the price, reduce the price or show him other cheaper cars. Without the missing information I would just flounder — like so many amateur salesmen do.

My friend Joe uses the "But?" tactic when promoting the Amway plan. Often he has prospects who say they want to earn more money or achieve certain goals and then they stop dead in their tracks. He picks up on their voice tone, looks at them quizzically and says "But?" They carry on, "*But* I'm not really into selling" or "*But* I don't think I could see myself selling soap." With the missing information he can immediately get to the heart of the problem. He can carefully guide and explain to his prospects exactly what they want to hear, clear up any misunderstandings or give further explanations.

When you ask people the right question and use "But?" you automatically get a complete and full picture of the customer's needs and desires. They actually describe and demonstrate the very answers they want. *They* tell *you* exactly what they want to hear. You must find out from your prospect exactly what he or she wants. Only when you have gathered sufficient information can you begin to sell to them. When you begin to sell him or her, match whatever it is you have to the reasons why he or she wants it.

All of the components of dynamic psychology are frighteningly powerful simply because they enable you to read your prospect and communicate with his or her inner world.

Before we discuss any more of the components of dynamic psychology, I want to talk about magic for a brief moment. For the purpose of this discussion I am going to assume you can't do magic. I want you to imagine the difficulty of making a rabbit appear, perhaps out of a hat, or maybe from nowhere. I want you to imagine making coins disappear and reappear at will. Any magician has had to practice these tricks to make them baffle and amuse people. Some tricks take months, even years, of practice in order for the magician to be able to bring them off smoothly, without a hitch. Practice, practice, practice is the secret of any magician. Selling is the closest thing I know to magic, and many times people have watched me conclude deals with certain individuals that other salesmen had previously said were impossible to deal with. These salesmen turn around to me and say, "I don't know how you do it. It's magic the way you sell," or "It's magic the way you get people to do what you want them to do." It is magic, I agree, but more to the point, it's practice, practice, practice, just like the magician. It is getting out in the field and talking with people and selling to people. I approach my selling as though I'm a magician, then I go one step further. I don't just do magic, I try to be magic. I try to bring magic into people's lives. You can do the same. Practice, practice, practice. Don't be frightened of using these powerful psychological tools. Everybody who is anybody has already been using them for years. Don't be a magician — be magic!

QUOTES — STORIES — SIMILES — METAPHORS

Sometimes, for many good reasons, it is necessary to say preposterous, loud or rude things to a prospect. Sometimes one has to be blunt, arrogant or very personal. Of course you can't do any of these things directly to your prospect if you want to get his or her money, but by using quotes, stories, similes or metaphors you can tell people anything to their faces and they'll never take offence. For example, as a business consultant I once had a client who kept interrupting me when I was telling him how to sort his business out. One day I said to him, "Last week I had a client in here who kept interrupting me, and I had to tell him to 'Shut up! Shut up! Shut up!' I'm so glad that *you* are not like *that*." My client never interrupted again, but he wasn't offended; he really did think I had had a previous client in who interrupted me. He was probably proud *he* wasn't like *that*!

My friend Joe uses a brilliant line when showing people the Amway plan for the second or third time. He sits down with the prospect and says, "Down the road I have this couple, they keep telling me of their dreams and plans, how they want this, how they want that, but they never take the first step to do anything. After a while you begin to wonder about the sincerity of people like that." The people he is talking to get motivated and start doing something, because they can see something of themselves in this lazy, insincere couple down the road. The reason why lines like this don't offend people is that they completely bypass the conscious mind. They go straight to the subconscious, which is the mind you, as a salesman, want to get at.

I once had a salesman who was so lazy it was beyond belief. He had great potential but he just wasn't using it. I decided to liven him up — subconsciously. I walked up to him, looked him in the eye, and said "I can't believe it. This guy came up to me this morning, looked me straight in the eye and said, *'You're the laziest person I know, what is the matter with you, why can't you get motivated? Just get out there and sell! sell! sell! You can do it! — Don't be lazy! — Get into action! — Do it now!'* Then he just walked off. What on earth would you do if some guy said that to you? I just don't know what to make of it!" With that *I* just walked off. The guy didn't know what had hit him. I had told him everything I wanted to, directly to his face, and he didn't even know it. Consciously, he thought someone had really said that to me. Subconsciously, he knew it was him. Within two short months, this salesman was turning in his best figures ever. I can't tell you how powerful the subconscious mind is. It's too powerful for mere words!

Making things sound as though it's not really you speaking to them gives you tremendous psychological leverage. This method of using quotes is a great way of trying out new behaviours on people and getting away with it. Analyse the results of your new behaviours and stick to the ones that work for you.

Let's go back to my consultancy office. Many times I have clients in front of me who are in bad financial shape, their businesses up against the wall. It is far less depressing to them, and also far more effective, if I liken their businesses to a ship. I talk about "sinking ship", "plugging up holes", "making the ship watertight", "bailing out", and "never abandoning the ship". These clients, more often than not, soon find themselves holding onto the tiller and steering the ship. The imagery reaches their subconscious minds. From what some of my prospects told me, they even went around their businesses as though they were a captain of a ship. They acted the way a captain would when saving his ship, and in doing so they saved their businesses. All they've done is subconsciously put themselves in charge instead of blaming everyone else. If they'd done that at the outset, their business might not have gotten into trouble.

Ben Feldman, who has a reputation for selling 100 million dollars' worth of life insurance a year, used a simile to conclude a certain policy sale. Feldman wanted to avoid talking about the prospect's own death and the need to provide for his survivors. What he did was to talk about Ernest Hemingway's death and the writer's estate, which was comparable to that of his prospect. Feldman went into detail about how Hemingway never bought insurance and how, as a result, his family suffered. This was a purposeful simile that allowed Feldman to touch on all the emotionally pertinent aspects of his prospect's death without forcing the prospect to *directly* confront his *own* death. Of course the prospect bought a policy.

You can tell anybody anything, providing you use these kinds of similes and stories. These sink right into people's subconscious minds. They even find themselves repeating the stories to other people.

I once had a guy who stubbornly refused to buy theft insurance for his car. Two of his cars had already been stolen; that put the premium even higher. As I left, I told him a simple story concerning a man in a woodcutting mill. A guy walked into the mill to find a machine operator holding his hand, from which blood was streaming. He was standing beside a huge circular saw. "Whatever happened to you?" said the first guy. The machine operator replied, "I cut a finger off on the saw. All I did was this — WHOOPS! — there goes another one." With that I left my prospect. The next day the guy called and asked me to write his theft policy for him, saying that he didn't want to lose any more fingers.

I once had in front of me a couple with various business problems. The business problems themselves were easy enough to sort out, but I could sense a more deeply rooted source of this couple's dilemma. The wife looked terrible, she had no makeup on and took no pride in her appearance. Her husband was equally bad, and on top of it all they had no respect for each other. I could hardly tell the couple, to their faces, what their real problem was without being offensive, so I told them about another similar couple I also had as clients. I purposely elaborated on how the woman took great pride in her appearance, how the husband loved her and how they respected each other. The way in which I told the story made it sound as though I was just talking about this other couple, not comparing them to the couple I had in front of me. The couple, transformed, retained me for a long period afterward, and to this day I'm convinced they never knew I got through to their subconscious minds.

CONDITIONED RESPONSE

Pavlov, the Russian physiologist (pronounced "fizzyologist") laid the groundwork for what is known as "conditioned response" with a series of experiments using dogs. Basically what Pavlov did was to ring a bell and then immediately give the dog some food. The "conditioned response" was that after a period of time the dog associated the bell with food and would salivate at the ring of a bell, whether or not food was presented.

People respond to many different kinds of things automatically because they have been conditioned over a period of many years to do so. Many people have been conditioned to lazy thinking, talking and communicating. Therefore, one of the first things you must do is get yourself a name that is easily pronounced and remembered. People have been conditioned to remember and respond to easy, catchy names. Nobody had heard of Cilla White until she changed her name to Cilla Black. Then she made her fortune singing beautiful songs. Adolf Schickelgruber would probably never have caused world havoc had he not changed his name to Adolf Hitler. Some names ring bells, others don't. A salesman called C. Stone changed his name when someone pointed out that there must be thousands of "C. Stones." He changed it to W. Clement Stone. And who would want to do business with "Jean Getty?" Surely J. Paul Getty strikes a more responsive chord. You have to have a name that rings a bell if you want fame and fortune. However, you might not have to go as far as the man who changed his name to "Exit" just to get his name up in lights!

Joe Girardi changed his name to Joe Girard and was named, twelve times, "The Greatest Salesman in the World" by the *Guinness Book of World Records*. You might have to change your name by knocking off an "i" at the end or change it completely. Whatever, it is very important. You may never have heard of Samuel Clemens, but you've almost certainly heard of Mark Twain. He had a specific reason for changing his name. So did Cassius Clay, who became Muhammed Ali. Leonard Slye changed his name and became the millionaire screen-cowboy Roy Rogers. You've got to have a name that rings a bell. I've shortened my name, from Ronald Lewis Maynard Holland to Ron Holland!

People have been conditioned into thinking that greatness is "high up" and failure is "lowdown." You have "the high and mighty," and "the lowest of the low." It was Freud who first used what is now known as Freud's Ploy. It is derived from the great psychoanalyst's couch. It puts the patient on a lower level than the psychiatrist. It also gives the impression of the patient having his feet in the air and the psychiatrist having his feet firmly on the ground. Why do you think they put the camera down low to shoot pictures of powerful characters in the movies or on television? It makes the person look higher, taller and more powerful.

This can help us in many ways. In my business consultancy office all the legs on all the chairs have been shortened by one inch. All except my own, that is. This gives the impression to the subconscious mind that I am higher and am in charge of the goings on. It's quite handy really, if you keep in mind that every single businessman who comes to me has to be told that he's been doing everything all wrong and I have to lead him into doing many new and different things.

Another time I use Freud's Ploy is when I'm selling. If I want to get tough, or put over a strong point, I sit higher than my prospect. I might have to sit on the office table or on the back of a chair to achieve this. I always seat myself higher than the other party if I want to dominate a conversation. However, there are also times when I may feel a prospect thinks I'm too pushy, so I will humble myself by getting lower than he is. Perhaps I'll sit on the bed, or maybe even on the floor. I move about, up and down, higher or lower, all depending on how the conversation is going and what kind of feedback I'm picking up from my prospect. I always seat myself to suit the occasion.

The majority of people in this world have inferiority complexes. The conditioned response is that everybody *thinks* he is the only one who feels inferior, because everyone else is conditioned to cover up his or her inferiority complex. Some people do have superiority complexes, but most of these cases are overcompensation: an inferiority complex turned inside out. I always *assume* the person sitting in front of me feels inferior. In establishing rapport I make absolutely certain he's not going to feel inferior when he's talking to me. I'll make sure I'm the underdog. When my prospect tells me about something he's accomplished, I'll never try to outdo him, the way so many amateurs do. I'll listen to him and respect everything he tells me. I will enthuse about his car, his home, his camera, his clothes, his work, garden, job and hobbies. My prospect is the man of the moment, and I'm going to make him feel great, important; I'll make him feel like a big, big man. For once in his life he's not going to feel inferior.

I will always be willing to be the butt of a joke. I'll be a clown, but not a fool. Everybody loves to laugh but nobody wants to do business with a fool, it insults his intelligence. In acting the clown rather than the fool, you will take people into your confidence. You'll be harmless, fun to be with. Now, I know you feel inferior, and it's hard to make yourself smaller than you already are. It's a paradox that to become larger than life, you must, initially, appear to be smaller than you really are.

ANCHORS

You have just read about conditioned response, i.e., the phenomenon where people respond automatically in a particular way to various things because they have been conditioned to do so over a *long* period of time.

Anchors are similar in nature, but unlike conditioned response, they can affect people in a very short space of time, in some cases hours, in others mere minutes or, in extreme cases, immediately.

Before I describe how you can use this manipulative tool, I want to show you some anchors that you already recognize. During a war, when someone suffers from shell shock, what happens is that he becomes "anchored" to a single blast or loud explosion. Even years later, if he hears a loud bang, the wartime memories come flooding back. A similar case is rape. A girl who has been raped is often anchored to the memory of someone touching her. Should anyone else touch her, all the feelings and emotions of the terrifying experience repeat themselves until, with time, the anchor wears off or she is treated by a psychiatrist. You could become anchored by a dog bite; if you do, any future meetings with dogs will bring back the fear of being bitten. A one-time experience can anchor you and bring back feelings or memories. A tune or song will often bring back fond memories, especially if you felt particularly happy or romantic at the time you first heard it. Many couples, on hearing a certain song will say "That's our song!" They've been anchored to it. Perfume can bring back memories of a particular girl or date, and the tone of someone's voice can also bring back an experience.

As long as a person is fully in touch with an experience he or she can be deliberately anchored to it by an external stimulus. You can recall that exact feeling in that person, at your command, simply by triggering the proper stimulus, the anchor. As far as we are concerned, an anchor is a method of being able to control and manipulate people's feelings and emotions at will.

There is no limit to the number of kinds of anchors, or to the experiences anchors can bring back. Anchoring is one of the most powerful and manipulative psychological tools that is used today by top salesmen and communicators.

I once got a bank manager to lend me vast amounts of money, unsecured, with the simple use of an anchor. I knew exactly what I wanted from this particular bank manager; I had been dealing with him for a number of years. For this particular application of the anchor I used an audible clearing of my throat. Every time I met with the bank manager I smiled and said how pleased I was to see him. As soon as I thought his inner feelings of happiness and glee were at their highest, I cleared my throat, more than loud enough for him to hear. On discussing mutually satisfactory deals, I would, whenever I felt his happy emotions were at the highest pitch, clear my throat with exactly the same sound. What I was doing was establishing an anchor whereby the bank manager would subconsciously begin to associate my throat clearing with his own good, positive feelings. Quite possibly the anchor took effect on the very first throat clearing, but since I was not in a particular hurry to close a deal I just kept reinforcing my anchor. On a few meetings jokes were told and I would again anchor the good positive feeling by audibly clearing my throat.

On the day I asked for a vast unsecured loan, I began my request, and ended my request, with a clearing of my throat. Sure enough my request was granted and the bank manager even went so far as to say that although it was against bank policy, he felt good about it.

You can use any method you like for anchoring. There is literally no end to the ways in which you can do it, but a few ways include: a handshake, a touch on the shoulder, a tap on the knuckle (kinesthetic); a wave of the hand, a nod of the head or a blinking of the eyes (visual); a clearing of the throat, a cough, a catch phrase or word (auditory); or a certain perfume or after-shave (olfactory).

At one time I employed a number of people in a large office. Every now and then morale would drop, as it does wherever people work together. On one particular occasion all the employees were gathered together and we were having a discussion. It was a very friendly discussion, and the camaraderie was particularly high. I told a very funny joke concerning three rabbits. I put particular, although subtle, emphasis on the word "rabbit" every time I said it. Everyone roared with laughter, and eventually the meeting dispersed. Thereafter, whenever morale dropped in the office, I would just stroll through and suddenly shout "Rabbits!" Of course, the morale would then automatically rise, because my employees had been anchored to the feelings of humour and happiness, and camaraderie, at the time of the rabbit joke. The triggering of the anchor "Rabbits!" brought these feelings back.

You can anchor people to a smell, a tone of voice, a wave of a hand, a scratch of the head, a facial expression or a noise. Many television personalities anchor audiences with a catch phrase. So powerful are these anchors, many people find themselves saying them in the same tone of voice as the television personality and eliciting the same happy response from people.

One anchor I used many times when I was a business consultant was rubbing my hands together with glee and saying "Money! Money! Money!" with lots of enthusiasm. I would anchor this as many times as possible to good or positive feelings that I got from my client. Whenever I sensed that my client's feelings had reached their fullest expression, I would anchor again, using exactly the same words and exactly the same tone of voice: "Money! Money! Money!" When it came to my client parting with a fee, he was obviously depressed, so at an appropriate moment I reminded him that he was now in the process of straightening his business out and soon he'd have a lot of money. I'd rub my hands together and say "Money! Money! Money!" This would bring his positive feeling back and all would be fine. It's very difficult to relieve people of money, if they don't feel happy or relaxed about it.

This kind of anchor is particularly good for getting people to part with money. In my experience it's one of the hardest things to do, but this psychological tool actually makes people feel good about it! As you can imagine, it's very handy to have someone happy, confident or enthusiastic just when you want him to be.

When using anchors you have to be aware of what you are doing. It would be no use at all if I were to anchor negative or depressed feelings. I would purposely generate positive, happy, enthusiastic responses from my clients and anchor those feelings when I felt they were at their highest pitch. You can tell by the brightness of people's eyes, their smile, tone of voice and relaxed posture that they are at their highest states of happiness and well-being.

Never underestimate the power of anchors — they work — they always have. It's just that you've never recognized them before. Don't be frightened of using the powerful manipulative tools outlined in this chapter. Use one at a time until you are proficient in its use. The ultimate success is found in using all of them on a prospect without even having to think about what you're doing. In other words, learn to use these manipulative tools *subconsciously*.

When I was selling insurance, I used the handshake as an anchor. What I would do was firmly shake the prospect's hand and at the same time boost his ego, saying how glad I was to meet him and anything else I could think of to put him on cloud nine. During my presentation, when we arrived at some point of mutual agreement, I would say "Well, at least that's one point we can shake on." You have probably met guys who are continually shaking hands, and this is what they are doing. By the third handshake my prospect is literally glowing because every time I shake his hand, back comes the feeling I implanted when we first met. On a few occasions I have failed to close a deal, shaken the prospect's hand to say goodbye, and there and then the positive feelings welled up inside and he said "Write up a policy!"

These anchors, like all psychological tools, are not easy to perceive. I guarantee that if you and I met tomorrow, and you even knew who I was and were looking out for anchors, you wouldn't recognize them. Furthermore, I guarantee I'd have an anchor on you within the first five minutes of meeting and you wouldn't know it.

One anchor I strongly advise you to establish for yourself is a self-motivation anchor. All you do is remember back to a time when you were self-motivated, when you actually got up and completed a task and were happy to do so. Remember this task in the fullest possible detail. See yourself doing whatever it was in your mind's eye. See it clearly, every detail in full colour. The success actually lies not in just remembering, but in actually imagining yourself back to that time. That's using your visual system. Now, hear all the relevant sounds and noises that happened while you were happily self-motivated. Talk to yourself internally about that whole remembered sequence. Make your experience lifelike, as though it were really happening to you now. Use your auditory system in every way you can think of. Now, feel each and every emotion of how you were when you completed this task. Use your kinesthetic system to its fullest degree. *Actually relive those feelings and emotions, don't just remember them.* Finally, recall any smells that were present. Use all four systems to the greatest extent possible. When all the systems are nearing their highest pitch, grasp your left wrist with your right hand and squeeze it. Squeeze the hardest when all your systems are at their peak. When you need to recall this feeling of self-motivation, use the anchor and squeeze your wrist with the exact pressure you applied when establishing the anchor and you'll be motivated to the same degree you were originally.

One salesman I trained in the use of psychological tools did brilliantly until we started to discuss the deliberate use of anchors. He argued, in essence, that it was preposterous to suggest that they work as simply as I described. His bone of contention was that if people can get anchored to mere touches and other equally simple things, they would go around *accidentally* anchoring and not knowing it.

I explained that unfortunately they do, and one of the most common examples is that of happily married couples who all of a sudden stop touching each other. What happens is that when a couple first get married, they hug and kiss and touch, and everything is great. Then, one day, the husband feels depressed, for no particular reason. Unwittingly, his wife comes up behind him, gives him a big hug and tells him to cheer up. Unfortunately she has anchored these actions to feelings of depression. When she next hugs her husband, suddenly these feelings come flooding back to him for no apparent reason. The anchor has taken hold, and he subconsciously associates his wife's hugs with the feelings of depression. For this very reason, I strongly advise you to only hug and kiss and touch when you are both in good, happy moods. Tragically, millions of married couples stop touching each other after being together a very short period of time simply because they anchored negative or depressed feelings.

By the time I had finished explaining this to the salesman, his face was ashen and his knuckles were white where he had been clenching his fists. He explained that that was exactly what had happened in his own marriage. I told him the remedy was ever so simple: I told him to go home, discuss it with his wife and make up. Once this kind of problem is brought into consciousness it is easily resolved.

When establishing anchors yourself, anchor only good, positive feelings and anchor them when they are at their highest pitch. Use a method that can be triggered only by you and remember that to bring back an anchored feeling in someone you have to use *exactly* the same stimulus you used when anchoring. For example, the audible clearing of your throat would have to sound exactly the same, or your handshake would have to be used exactly the same way, and the amount of pressure the same, in order to trigger the anchor.

THE NEGATIVE SELL

I don't like talking about closing deals, but dynamic psychology is the most powerful way in the world to close deals and make people buy from you.

The negative sell has been used for thousands of years and human nature always falls for it. It is the ultimate close and, in using it, you protect yourself at the same time against buyer's remorse. You are probably familiar with the boy-girl tactic known as "playing hard to get." The harder it is to get the girl, the more desirable she becomes. Thus, the more you tell your customer "not to buy, but check out other cars first," or "slow down and compare prices with other insurance companies before you buy our policy," the more you take him into your confidence and the more convinced he is that he is making the right deal with you.

Like all dynamic psychology there is more to the negative sell than meets the eye. One salesman will tell his prospect to check out other cars before making up his mind and the prospect will end up buying from him. Another salesman tells his prospect to check out other cars before making up his mind. The prospect will do just that and never come back again! Well, what is it the super, super salesman *does* to actually close these deals, when to the casual observer it would appear that he is trying his hardest *not* to sell?

We have already seen how to sell, and how to establish subconscious rapport, basically by selling with the same processing system our prospect has and behaving the way he does. It automatically follows that if we want to break that rapport and alienate ourselves from our prospect, we sell to the wrong processing system and stop behaving like our prospect.

A simple illustration of negative selling a car would be something like this: the prospect is an Auditory, therefore you have put great emphasis on the purr of the engine, the squeal of the radials, the quietness of the door shutting, the high quality stereo radio and the swishing sound of the electric windows. You have also established subconscious rapport with your prospect. You speak in the same tone of voice and in the same way he or she does. You also mirror his or her behaviour. You know you've really got the prospect hooked on the car. Now you want to really take the prospect into your confidence and close the deal. You say, "Look, why don't you go and see if the other dealer, John Doe, has any cars that look good to you, see if anything he has to offer looks the part. You might get a better picture by comparing his cars with ours." You say all this in a very sincere manner and in a genuine way. The customer will buy from you without even going to the other dealer. Why? What did you say? Well, for a start you used a slightly different tone of voice to break the rapport. You also stopped behaving like the prospect, and last, but not least, you negative sold by an almost exclusive use of visual words when your prospect was an Auditory. Although the prospect consciously heard you tell him or her one thing, it didn't mean a bit to the prospect because there was no rapport.

For these very same reasons I have seen an amateur salesman sell a car one minute, and talk the customer out of it the next. Within the next half hour he had talked the guy back into taking the car, but his final move convinced the prospect to go and have a look at the cars at another dealer's. The customer went, and our amateur salesman never saw him again.

Some prospects actually need to bring up objections before they buy anything. In overcoming these objections you make your goods even more desirable to that prospect.

Other prospects are turned off immediately by salesmen who come on too strong. On one occasion I sensed that a guy who was looking at some used cars thought I was being too pushy. One car particularly interested him. However, when he asked the price of the car, I negative sold him. I told him that I didn't think the car was for sale, because we had only just bought it and it was such a good car that the boss wanted it for himself. That made the prospect really eager. He then had to *buy* the car from me, instead of me selling it to him. I can't emphasize strongly enough the importance of flexible behaviour.

For some prospects, putting things out of reach immediately makes the goods become more desirable. Everybody you deal with has to be treated in a different way and if you are not getting the desired response then you must alter your behaviour.

This also holds true when motivating people. Generally speaking, if you give praise and encouragement, you can motivate most people. However, it hasn't escaped my attention that this doesn't work for all people. You may have to be negative in order to get positive results. With one salesman I tried everything, and got nowhere, until I was negative. I told him I didn't think he'd ever make a good salesman. I just didn't think he had it in him. I went on and on, negative! negative! negative! In the end, he got so fired up he just had to prove me wrong — so he went out and sold! sold! sold!

A GOOD SERVICE OR PRODUCT

Many times I failed in business because I had come up with a product or service that was not up to par. I thought that because I was a Number One salesman I could talk anybody into anything. I could usually unload a few useless gizmos or worthless widgets onto some unsuspecting buyers, but you can't fool all of the people all of the time. The product or service has to be good in every respect. All the top class Number One super, super salesmen I have met or studied or read about sold a good product or service. If it wasn't a good one to begin with they would modify it until it was.

If anybody were to ask me what the definition of a good product was, I would have to reply that a good product is a product of the subconscious mind. This does not imply that you have to design or manufacture the product yourself. What it does mean is that the product you are selling is right because your subconscious mind *tells* you it is right — right for you to sell at a particular time in your life. You will never be short of the right product to sell if you faithfully follow the earlier chapters in this book. You have been shown the way to create Eurekas! which are foolproof ideas for success. This chapter shows you how to sell them and convert them into money.

But now that you know how to sell, the question of price resistance arises. Price resistance amounts to about 60 percent of all resistance factors. The problem of price resistance is easily overcome if you recognize it. I find it is a psychological advantage if I get it in first. You see, in doing this, you minimize the problem and don't forget the problem is there, whether you like it or not, whether the prospect brings it up or you do. If I bring up the price factor first, the prospect automatically relaxes, because the problem is out in the open, even if not yet resolved. The problem soon will be resolved because I understand this price resistance barrier and I have done my homework. I put my sales story across logically. Now here is an interesting fact. I find it beneficial to point out any bad things about the deal as well as the good things. In doing so I find the prospect is even happier than if I had only mentioned the good things. However, my main effort is to *concentrate* on the good things, while not making a big deal of the bad ones.

I never rush a sales pitch. I am never in a hurry to get away from my prospect. As far as he is concerned, I have all the time in the world. Even if I have a dozen appointments awaiting me, I will not rush him. Selling is not a hit and run business. It is an art.

If the sale has been carried out using all of the components here, in a conversational manner, the deal will close itself.

ZOOM SECRETS!

1. You have now discovered one of the greatest success secrets of all time. It is simply this: the super, super salesmen establish subconscious rapport before they even try to sell a prospect.
2. People process information either auditorily, kinesthetically or visually. By selling to the processing system that your prospect uses, you make your goods and ideas maximally acceptable to him or her.
3. If you read your prospect carefully, you will find he or she will tell you, subconsciously, all the answers to the things you need to know.
4. There is magic involved in telling a prospect everything he or she wants to hear. Simply ask the right questions and listen to the answers, and you will then be able to tell your prospect what he wants to hear.
5. By using quotes and stories you can tell anybody anything without offending them. Furthermore, in doing so you get through to the subconscious mind.
6. Get yourself a catchy name that is easily pronounced and remembered. When talking to people, alter your seating position in relation to them according to whether you want to dominate the situation or humble yourself. A powerful psychological tool is to assume that *everyone* you are dealing with has an inferiority complex.
7. Use anchors to bring back positive, good and happy feelings both in yourself and others.
8. Some prospects need to raise objections before they can buy anything. It is part of their psychological makeup. Also, some people need to be told that they can't do things before they will be motivated into action.
9. It's obvious really, but you must have a good service or product to sell, no matter how good a salesman you are. Unfortunately, people still insist on trying to make fortunes out of rubbish. You can't fool all of the people all of the time.

CHAPTER 7

ACTION IS POWER

*"Action makes more
fortunes than caution."*

VAUVENARGUES

After so much discussion about taking time out
for meditation, S.S.S., and the achievement of action
through non-action, we have to be very careful not to
be contradictory. Make no mistake, Action is Power,
but the kind of action the majority of people indulge
in isn't. Action will only be powerful when it is the
right action. Right actions come as a result of following the Eurekas! from the subconscious mind. Eurekas! will come to those who get into action with the
ideas and tools they possess at hand, providing they
are taking time out to meditate in S.S.S. and spend
a certain amount of time visualizing every day.

Even with all the meditation, S.S.S., Eurekas! and
Will Power in the world, if you do not act, you will not

achieve. The action may not be a Herculean task, but act you must. Using the subconscious mind along the lines we have been discussing, you cannot help but come up with the most devastating and illuminating ideas for success. If you do not act on the ideas the subconscious mind gives you, nothing will happen. As Emerson proclaimed, "Only do the thing and then you shall have the power." The doing and the power go together.

Imagine baking a cake but leaving out one of the vital ingredients, perhaps baking powder. The cake would not rise, it would be a flop. So it is with a success philosophy. Leave out an ingredient and nothing happens. Leave out action and you are a non-starter. Time is your enemy, it is not on your side. We all get these flashes of inspiration, the Eurekas!, and tomorrow always seems the appropriate time to put them into action. This reminds me of the little boy who came running past me the other day, puffing and panting, almost out of breath. He ran up and over the railway bridge and down the other side, only to see the train disappear in the distance. The porter smiled and said, "If you'd run faster, son, you would have caught it." The boy replied, "I ran fast enough, sir, but I just didn't start soon enough." Action is the vital, key factor in your search for wealth.

While you were at the pictures, Ray Kroc got into action and bought a single hamburger stand in California from the McDonald Brothers and turned it into a $500 million fortune. I might also add he was 52 years old when he started. You have the knowledge to start now, and don't forget, *now* spelled backwards is *won*! The power is in the things we have not done, the friends we have never made, the love we have not used, the ideas we have never acted on. Had we done these things, we would have had the power. *Action! Action! Action!* I ought, therefore I can.

Colonel Harlan Sanders, of Kentucky Fried Chicken fame, got into action when he was over 65 and retired. Kentucky Fried Chicken franchises sold in America, Canada, Britain and Japan. Even more significant is the fact that over one hundred businessmen who got into action became millionaires by buying the Kentucky Fried Chicken franchise. Within ten years Kentucky Fried Chicken sales were over one hundred million dollars a year. Sanders conceived an idea and acted on it. He did all this while you were lounging on the beach, or was it playing cards over at Pat's house? Perhaps you were watching television, oh no, you remember: you were at the bar, with ten million cousins.

Benjamin Disraeli once said "Life is too short, to be little." Why is it, then, we all sit around and wait for the right time to act? The time is always right when the subconscious mind hands us an idea. Follow it through to the letter, even if it seems illogical at that time. It is there and then that you must act on it.

It is only when we allow ourselves to be led by someone else or do something our conscious mind tells us to do that things go wrong. The subconscious mind never makes a mistake. Action will be in the form of talking, persuading people to help you, to lend you money or to buy your goods. Once your subconscious mind has handed you the plan, you literally *Talk and Grow Rich*.

There can be no excuse for not getting into action. Limited education, present situation in a humble trade, or lowly means cannot be accepted as excuses. The most inspiring and successful speaker the world has ever seen began life as a lowly carpenter. He died on a cross on a hill nearly two thousand years ago, and his name will never be forgotten.

When your friends tell you that you can't do this, that, or the other because you are only a carpenter or a shop assistant or a cashier or a waiter, just remember that there is no such thing as "only a carpenter."

Now, I must be honest with you — I have never had any trouble inspiring people into action for the *first* time, and launching them into new and exciting lives and fields of endeavour. The difficult bit is to inspire people who have genuinely tried and failed, not once, but many times. They lose confidence, become demoralized and depressed, tired, and give up. This happens so often that I have devoted an entire chapter to failure.

An undergraduate at Harvard was lying on the grass by the campus when a professor approached him and asked what he was doing. "Oh, just killing time," replied the student. "I think you are wrong," said the teacher. "Time is killing you!" Never kill time. There is so much you can do. Yes, even without money!

While you were playing frisbee, Robert Ringer was out there selling real estate. While you were playing darts with Joe, Charles and Elsie Marsh were having a meeting. While you were reading the evening paper, Chuck and Jean Strehli were having *another* meeting! You were fishing (you never caught anything) while Joe Girard was selling cars, and while you were packing up the tackle, Edna Larsen was making her tenth cosmetic sale of the day.

The evening you were restless and kicked around a dozen different notions but just couldn't get your act together, W. Clement Stone worked away at his insurance business until 11:30, just the way he does most evenings (with a second shift of typists and secretaries).

While you were at that yard sale wasting money on junk, Joe M. Gandolfo was on the telephone selling life insurance. While you were window shopping, Bernice Hansen was having a meeting, and while you were watching the ball game on television, Mary Hudson was buying up gas stations.

You only get out of life what you put in, and I think this little verse conveys the secret well.

A Simpleton walked into the bank
And said with the greatest of ease,
"I'd like to draw out a thousand dollars
In twenty dollar bills, if you please."
The cashier replied, "Ah, well, well,
You must pardon me sir, if I grin.
But you cannot take anything out
For you haven't put anything in."

With all the will in the world you cannot sit down and invent a brilliant idea like the skateboard, the hula hoop, a troll doll, a gonk, hamburgers, dunkin' donuts, comic books or any other great money maker. We know beyond a shadow of a doubt that great ideas come to us when we are not thinking. The secret, then, is to act on our own ideas when they do come. Now here is the quirk of the subconscious mind. It gives us ideas so clever, so easy, so profitable, so big, so exciting, so terrific that we tend to shy away from them and shelve them. You think the idea is so clever that there must be something wrong with it. You think the idea is so simple somebody else would have done it and so profitable it just can't be true and, true for you! Well, let me tell you, maybe you are right, someone else did think of these ideas, but they probably thought in the same way as you, and never activated them. Think of this book for a moment. Napoleon Hill's *Think and Grow Rich* has been on the market for more than thirty years. It is a renowned international best seller and is known as the "classic" of motivational books. The obvious sequel is *Talk and Grow Rich*. Hundreds, even thousands, of people must have had that idea come to them, as ideas do. But nobody acted, except me!

Do something, even if it is only an act. Make a start with the tools you have and better tools will come along. To quote an ancient English proverb: "Everyone must row with the oars he has." So many people wait for this, for that or for the other, saying, "Everything comes to those who wait." As far as I am concerned, the only thing that comes to those who wait is death!

My favourite poem is by Harvey Scott, and you could do no better than to learn it.

> I saw the old thief, Father Time,
> Come hirpling down the road;
> He had a sack upon his back,
> Lost minutes were his load.
> He opened it and showed to me
> Not minutes, but a host
> Of years, decades, a century
> Or more of minutes lost.
> "I want to buy a year," I said
> "And I shall pay you well."
> "If this earth's mould were finest gold,
> To you I would not sell,
> For I have minutes stolen from Kings,
> From Milton, Shakespeare, Bach,
> How could you buy such precious things,
> Your common gold is trash."
> He tied his sack and said, "Farewell,
> Young man, I've got my fee."
> For while I tried to make him sell,
> He stole an hour from me!

Get into action immediately, and talk, talk, talk. Talk to young people, ask about the latest trends, fads, and crazes. Talk to them, ask what they do in their leisure hours. Mix with them, generate an awareness of what is going on about you. Many a profitable idea is based on fun toys for kids. How is that some people have magnificent houses, exotic cars and entertain their friends lavishly? Are they doing something you are not, are they getting into action? I have already told you the power is in the things we have not done. Force yourself to act.

In England, there is a classic story about a hustler. The tale is set in the hills of Cumbria, many years ago. The story has it that a hustler knocked on the door of a farmhouse to scrounge some milk and a few eggs. An old lady answered the door and gave him the eggs and milk he had asked for. He was well known in the district, and he wasn't particularly surprised when the old lady invited him in for coffee. Once inside the farmhouse, the old lady pointed out through the kitchen window to her lovely daughter, who was at the time feeding the chickens. The girl had an hourglass figure, long blonde hair and a pretty face. "If you take my daughter's hand in marriage," the old lady told him, "you can have the farm and the money we have in the bank." The hustler gulped down his coffee, fled the farmhouse and drove his horse and cart back to his mother's dilapidated cottage. When the hustler told his mother of the incident, they were both of the same opinion. There must be a catch; they would be sure to lose something. They spent many hours puzzling over this but came to no conclusion. Some years later, the hustler was in the same area and again came across the farmhouse where the incident took place, although by that time he had forgotten all about it. He knocked on the door to ask for some eggs and to his surprise the beautiful daughter opened it. His mind raced back and he remembered her mother asking him to take the daughter's hand in marriage, the farm and the money. Curious, the hustler could not help asking, "What was the catch, all those years ago, when your mother asked me to marry you?" The girl replied, "No catch at all, I simply fell in love with you, but was too shy to get to know you. So my mother asked for me. Alas, she is dead now and I myself have married the farmer on yonder farm." The hustler walked away, numbed by his experience. You see, the hustler had nothing, nothing at all, he never did have. When he was offered the girl's hand in marriage, the farm, the money in the bank, all he could think of was, "What was the catch, what would he lose?" The moral of the story is: WHEN YOU HAVE EVERYTHING TO GAIN, AND NOTHING TO LOSE, DO IT NOW.

Tragedy lies in the hundreds of thousands of highly educated young men and women worldwide who are unemployed. They have degrees, knowledge, potential power, but they do nothing. They are waiting for the right job to come along, the right opportunity, they only want to do what they like doing. Opportunities come and go and still they do nothing.

Many years ago an old sage told an aspiring yogi that a "touchstone" would be worth a lot of money to him, for it was diamond encrusted in gold. The "touchstone" looked like any other pebble to be found on any shore, the only difference was that the "touchstone" would be warm, whereas all the other pebbles would be cold. The yogi set out in search of his fortune, looking for a "touchstone." He scoured beach after beach, shore after shore. He picked up pebbles by the score, by the hundred, by the thousand, and as he felt each one and it was cold, he tossed it back into the sea. One day he happened to pick up a stone that was without question a "touchstone," for it was definitely warm. However, the yogi was so used to tossing the pebbles back into the sea that he tossed this one back also. In the same way, we go through life not grasping the opportunities that reveal themselves as the "touchstone" did. We still toss them away, for it is our long-standing tradition, our force of habit, our second nature, to toss opportunities away, fail to recognize them and to look only for the catch. As you go through life, let this be your goal: look for the doughnut, not the hole!

There is so much to do, when you know what to do, where to start, even without any money. The power is in the things we have not done. All the lethargic, idle people; the dull, dreary, dreamy beings; the inert and inactive — all these people can succeed in their endeavours by doing the things they have not done. If you have a beard, shave it off; if you have not got a beard, grow one; if you drive to work, go by bus. Repetition and routine kill. If you never write to friends, now is the time. If you don't have any friends, make some. If you go to dances, stop going. Do something different. If you don't go to dances, you must go to one tonight. Remember, *tonight*, not tomorrow!

Do something different, get up and go, even if you are not sure of where you are going. Dr. Joost A. M. Meerloo said, "Change and growth of personal outlook is one of the most important scientific findings in psychology and is agreed on by all psychologists." These things don't need thinking about, they need doing. If a war hero were to think before he jumped out of a trench to advance, he would retreat instead! Heroes act on impulse, they do things, they don't think about them. Spontaneous action is the name of the game. It is less often the results of a mistake than the stress caused by prolonged indecision that is the most harmful. Indecision kills. Don't be indecisive, just get up and go. In the U.S. Infantry manual there is a line about decision: "Any plan, no matter how poorly conceived, if boldly executed is better than inaction." Make a note in your diary that the man of indecision can't be started; the man of decision can't be stopped. Make the decision today that you are going to be a man of decision and a man of action.

Change all the furniture around in the house, get a different car, take up raquetball or squash. If you wear casual clothes in the evenings, change to a suit, and vice versa during the day. The power is in the things we have not done. Instead of doing the clubs every night, do some meditation in S.S.S. Get time on your own for a change, and I mean on your own.

It is doing the same things, in the same ways, day in and day out, that stifles our initiative to action. If we're in a routine, if we're not used to acting when the subconscious presents us with a Eureka!, then we won't act when we do get a great idea. Start today, make no delay. First get the study or spare room ready for your own silent meditation. Then get all your best clothes ready, put them on, and go see someone you have not seen for a long time, even if it is their turn to come and see you. If you have ever fancied the idea of doing something different, do it. Parachuting, flying, waterskiing, skin-diving, whatever takes your fancy, do it today. All this has absolute bearing on, and control over, your ability as a successful salesman. You are hardly likely to approach an unknown person or business if you will not even get up and do the things you really want to do. Talk to the waiter, the newspaper man, talk to the person sitting next to you on the train. Tell him what you would like to do, ask him what he does and what he would like to do. Never be in too much of a hurry not to leave time for talking to all these people. You see it all the time, every day in every street; a man dashes up to the newspaper boy, shoves a quarter in his hand, takes a paper and dashes off again. Where has it got him? The difference is between action and hurry. They are worlds apart. This is where the big mistake is made. Action builds and progresses. Hurry and haste destroy the mind, body and soul.

All the millionaires' lives that I have studied in minute detail have a common denominator. They want money and go after it, and they recognize money doesn't have legs — *they* go to *it*. They realize that to hunt elephant you wouldn't go to New York, you would go to Africa or India. In the same vein they go where the money is and make it theirs. They realize that the perfect time for action never comes. There are always problems of inflation, bad economies, wars, lack of capital, the wrong staff, flooded markets, always something to contend with. Because they know the time is never perfect, they act now, with the tools and ideas they have at hand. They know that given quietness and time, the subconscious mind will assimilate all the knowledge and facts it has at hand and create its own brilliant idea.

While you were out bowling, Aristotle Onassis was buying two hundred thousand ton oil tankers, and while you were lying in the chaise lounge just longing for something exciting to happen, J. Paul Getty was buying up oil stock.

These millionaires are not afraid of failure. If they do fail, they once again get into action and bounce back even harder. Dr. William J. Reilly recognized this and wrote, "The only person who makes no mistakes is the person who does nothing and that is the greatest mistake of all."

The secret, then, is to start changing the smaller things and doing the smaller things. The bigger things will follow, believe me. I know because it is exciting and wonderfully true.

Where do you start you may well ask. Do the duty that lies nearest you, the next duty will then become clearer. Even putting to use wasted minutes can be enough to make the difference between success and failure. Do you realize that if you are an average American you waste fifty money making days every year by drinking coffee? The average coffee break extends to 35 minutes. Two of these breaks every day add up to fifty 8-hour days a year, all wasted! There's something for you to ACT ON!

A situation that I was involved in when I was a used car salesman illustrates that Action is Power particularly well. As an Apprentice Millionaire, I was involved in many money-making schemes, and of all of these, the used car business taught me the most. You see, when you are selling used cars you come into contact with every conceivable type of person. Doctors, lawyers, drug addicts, labourers, carpenters, nurses, teachers, you name the vocation, they all buy cars. Also you meet different types of personalities and during a period of time every buying, selling, part exchange, and warranty claim situation arises. And each deal has to stand on its own feet in order to turn a profit.

The incident I refer to involved a used car site where I was learning the trade of the Apprentice Millionaire. The sales manager placed an advertisement for a salesman. The first salesman arrived and quit after the first day. He left a note addressed to the sales manager to the effect that if the company were to spend $5,000 on advertising, $50,000 on more stock and $10,000 on painting and decorating the site he might consider staying on. He pointed out that only a few prospects browsed through the few cars on the site.

The following day another salesman arrived. Boy, did I learn a lot from him. His attitude was, "Never mind the wheeling and dealing, let's get on with the ducking and diving!" He did, too! His favorite word was "sharp". He got in at 7 a.m. sharp and immediately proceeded to make the place look sharp. Each car was carefully wiped over with a chamois cloth to clear off the overnight dust and dew. Every car was started, its battery charged and its interior made impeccably clean. What I learned from this salesman I not only applied to the car business but to all my businesses and to life in general. He made particularly sure each car would start; there is almost nothing that will kill a deal faster (after a customer shows interest) than having a car fail to start when it comes to the test drive.

This super, super salesman taught me how to have everything running, sharp, organized and efficient so that when a customer did put in an appearance we would be ready for him. Together we made a sharp little label for each car key and hung it up on a board so that one could immediately find the right key to the car in question. Next, we would sharpen up the office;

making sure all finance forms and documentation were readily available.

To generate more stock without capital outlay we would phone around to other dealers and see if they had any excess stock that they would allow us to sell on a split profit basis. Sometimes they did, sometimes they didn't. However, the point is we were now doing something to improve business. We were getting into action! We didn't stop there. Every day we made sure that we did at least two positive things to improve the business, even if it was phoning people we knew to see if they wanted cars, cleaning the showroom windows, sending out a few pieces of mail or changing the position of the cars around on the site. This attitude of "Do something" can and must be adopted no matter what your vocation. Money can be, and is, generated not necessarily with capital, but with action. Also, when your Eureka! presents itself, although it will be a foolproof idea for success, nothing will happen without action. John Wanamaker wisely said "Nothing comes merely by thinking about it."

While you were thinking I was setting up seven motorcycle shops and while you were sleeping I was running my consultancy business. While you were "just out for a drive" I was developing property and while you were browsing in the antique shops I was *selling* antiques. While you are reading this book I'm not only out in the field selling it, but I'm also writing another book! And as soon as I'm done with that, I'll write another.

Henry Ford was a true believer that Action is Power. When there was a problem in his business, whether it was on the shop floor or in the accounts department or in the tool shop, he did not send for the person who was in charge of that particular department, *he* went and saw *them!* When he was asked why he should go to the trouble spot instead of summoning someone to explain, he replied, "It saves time, I can get away from the other fellow a lot faster than he can leave me!'' Ford gave the world a dependable, economical automobile, and it didn't happen by accident. My feeling is that Henry Ford used the words of A. W. Robertson as his motto. ''If a man does only what is required of him, he is a slave. The moment he does more, he is a free man.''

You can see the necessity for action. You can see that even when the Coca-Cola Syrup Company had bought and paid for the great idea ''BOTTLE IT,'' they still had to get into action and bottle it. But, sadly, most people stand around, killing time, worrying about trivia and thinking about things gone by, instead of acting now in preparation for a better future.

When Will Rogers said, ''Don't let yesterday use up too much of today,'' he had more or less the same thing on his mind that Alexander Woollcott had when he said, ''Many of us spend half our time wishing for things we could have if we didn't spend our time wishing.'' You must cultivate the awareness that I keep telling you about. Time and action. Until you appreciate fully the significance of these words, you are doomed to remain a man of mediocrity. Don't forget that I only drink to genius.

A last scene you might consider is that you are lying on your deathbed. You have lived your life and have only a few seconds to live. The thoughts that rush through your mind may well be something like: ''If only I'd asked that girl out, if only I'd talked to Mr. O'Keefe and tried to sell him my ideas, if only I'd followed through with my ideas, if only I'd done whatever it was I wanted to do, for now I know, although it's too late, that nobody in the whole world would or could have stopped me.''

Put your hat on and Go!

ZOOM SECRETS!

1. No matter how many brilliant Eurekas! you have, if you don't follow through on them with action, nothing will happen. As Emerson said, "Only do the thing and then you shall have the power."
2. You can start your action campaign by getting the spare room ready for your own private meditation.
3. If you have ever wanted to do something different, do it: parachuting, flying, water-skiing, skin diving; whatever catches your fancy, do it today. Print the message onto your subconscious that you are a man or woman of action.
4. Don't waste fifty days a year, as the average American does, drinking coffee — get into action instead!
5. Each deal has work to be done on it before it can be sold. Never mind the wheeling and dealing, get on with the ducking and diving!
6. Instead of watching the television, sitting around *waiting* for something to happen, why don't you get into action and *make* something happen?

CHAPTER 8

POWER FAILURE

"You're on the road to success when you realize that failure is merely a detour."

WILLIAM G. MILNES, JR.

Most of us have heard the saying: "With every failure comes a seed of benefit, twice the size of adversity, if you look for it." We understand that if we make mistakes we can profit by them, and not make them again. Why is it, then, that so many salesmen, entrepreneurs, executives and, in fact, people from all walks of life, fail to attain their goals, fail to make the grade, and fail to become successful!

Although people realize that there is in the experience of failure a potential for learning something about power, they do not know how to go about it. When their first business venture fails they shrug their shoulders, laugh it off and somehow or other manage to start again. However, the next time around different mistakes are made, sometimes through no fault of the individual entrepreneur, but again failure is the end result. Only this time it is just a little bit harder to start again, a little bit harder to gain self-confidence and a little bit harder to get onto even the first rung of the ladder. Things become more difficult with each succeeding failure. Finally, the motto becomes "I've tried and failed, so what's the point?"

Many of us as children had strict upbringings and were probably taught, among other things, to care — to care about this, to care about that. If you said in front of your parents "I don't care," you probably got drummed into you this verse or a similar one:

> Don't Care was made to care,
> Don't Care was hung,
> Don't Care was put in prison,
> And made to play the drum.

Very catchy, I agree, but too much of this sort of brainwashing nullifies the aggression we need for success. (Note carefully that "aggression" does not mean "over-aggression", which is just as fatal to success as timidness). We care too much about what people think about us, and it is only when we "don't give a damn" that we can get on the road to riches, fame and fortune. We are frightened of criticism should we fail and this is in direct opposition to the "don't give a damn" attitude we need for success. Gabriele d'Annunzio, the man who helped unite the state of Italy, even had a mascot of a Buddha that he wore around his neck. It bore the inscription "*I don't care a damn*."

Many of the young fighter pilots who fought in World War II had no nerves, no fear, they "didn't care a damn". In many instances they were told to "consider yourselves already dead". Only when they adopted the attitude of not caring did they become successful fighter pilots. In a similar way you must adopt this same attitude to become successful in your life's work.

When you fail — as is inevitable, for success is built on failure — I want you to remember Winston Churchill, that great orator, smashing his stick on the floor and saying "Never, never, never, never give up!!!" You can see how the British were motivated into action against the so-called "greatest fighting force ever assembled in the history of time."

Centuries ago, Aesop told the tale of two frogs, who, in their travels, came across a large bowl of cream. They hopped up onto the rim of the bowl and the inevitable happened, they fell in. Within a short space of time, one of the frogs was overcome by the mass of white creamy substance and drowned. The other frog, however, just would not give up, he beat his arms and legs about, he struggled and he fought. He would not submit. After a while the cream turned into thick butter, and he hopped out.

When Abraham Lincoln was at his wits' end and the pressure was really on, he was often heard to say "This too will pass." It always does. Five hundred years before Christ was born, Heraclitus said, "Nothing is permanent but change." Things are always changing, failure is only a passing phase. Edison failed over ten-thousand times before he succeeded in producing the electric light. Can you say that you have failed ten-thousand times? Of course you can't!

Soichiro Honda was nearly bankrupt when he decided to go into the motorcycle market. Within a few years he captured more than half of the European and American market. Persistence won through again. Walt Disney did go bankrupt, but he kept on. Today the Disney empire grosses well in excess of three-hundred-million dollars a year.

If you have studied English history, you may remember Robert Bruce. He was in hiding, worried and trying to work out his strategy for fighting the British at the Battle of Bannockburn. He watched a spider trying to make a web. However hard the spider tried he could not spin the gossamer to form a web he was trying to weave between two pillars. The spider would not give up, he kept on trying. Robert Bruce was amazed at this persistent little fellow. Eventually, as if by magic, the spider succeeded, he spun his web; he attained; he won! Bruce coined the phrase, "If at first you don't succeed, try, try, try again." It was this experience that helped him through his failures. Success is achieved and maintained by those who try and keep on trying. I quote from Elbert Hubbard's *Note Book:* "There is no failure except in no longer trying."

Everybody has a multitude of friends when they begin to be successful. However, the minute someone fails, the friends disappear. The smiles and smirks on friends' faces are not figments of your imagination when you fail. They are actually pleased. It brings you back down to their level. It was Orson Welles who wrote in *The New York Times*, "When you are down and out, something always turns up, and it is usually the noses of your friends." Expect it and ignore it. This is your persistence test, the one you have to pass many, many times before you succeed. As you know, I have devoted much time, study and research into success, and why and how men become rich and successful. In retrospect, I find I know more about failure than success, for every successful man has failed many more times than he has succeeded.

I have failed many times and I am not ashamed to admit it. I purposely cultivated a thick skin, impervious to failure. It was either that or be an "also ran," which was not for me. When things got tough, and they often did, I used to think of the cockroach. These little fellows go back in time over five hundred million years, and they are still with us. When you consider all the species that have become extinct in that period of time it makes you wonder. Scientists have proven cockroaches are impervious to atomic radiation, and they have survived heat, cold, famine, drought and floods. One experiment was done in which five cockroaches were put in a sealed jar for a complete year without food or water. At the end of the year the lid was removed. The cockroaches had not eaten each other or died; they had lowered their metabolic rate to the lowest possible level in order to survive. Let us remember then that however small and humble we are, we too can be individually unassailable, and I am convinced that a thick skin helps. The Yogis practice something of a nature similar to what the cockroaches did. They can suspend their breathing, lower their metabolic rate and stop their hearts, if they want to. They often do this in conjunction with spiritual attainment. When you empty your mind in your meditation, you are putting up a psychic shield by blocking out thoughts of failure and in doing so protecting yourself from negative influences.

When people who were once your friends come up to you and say, spitefully, "Well, what are you going to do now that you have failed and have no money?" or "I did try and warn you that you were out of your league," you can look straight through them and know inwardly that you are progressing in the right direction. There can be no success without failure, for failure is one of the main ingredients of success.

In your studies as a Student of Success, you must read biographies not only of great businessmen, world leaders, tycoons, and entrepreneurs, but also those of mountaineers, lone yachtsmen, racing drivers and scientists, for there you will discover what persistence really is, what keep on keeping on is really all about. You must adopt this pioneer attitude, the "don't give a damn what people think" attitude, if you are going to attain.

Edward Bok truthfully stated, "Poverty is the richest experience that can come to man," an experience which, however, he strongly advises one to get away from as quickly as possible. I know you are have lost your identity and self-confidence. You must keep up the fight to re-establish your self-esteem. Only then will you feel better, only then will you begin to be a success again. Nothing succeeds like success. It is the first rung of the ladder we must get on, the first step we must take forward. The next time you get a bit depressed, a little more anxious than you should, consider this couplet:

> I used to cry because I had no shoes,
> Until in the street I met a man who had no feet.

One of the most common causes of failure is "trying to get a quart out of a pint." Many people do it unwittingly all the time. Their life styles, automobiles, clothes and credit accounts all run far in excess of what their businesses actually net. If one must spend a lot, one must first ensure that one's business actually produces sufficient income to pay for the extravagances out of the profit, not merely out of the cash flow. Face up to these facts and understand them well if you are to succeed. In front of your eyes is the sure-fire formula for failure: *spend more than you earn.*

When Wall Street crashed on Tuesday, October 29, 1929, great losses and financial disaster struck many Americans. One millionaire lost every dollar he had, his entire fortune. He decided to commit suicide by drowning himself, the strain was too much for him. He took himself down to the beach. As he reached the water's edge, however, he bent down and picked up a beautiful, delicate seashell. The ruined millionaire pondered on this shell and thought if such a fragile shell could survive rough seas that sank thousands of tons of shipping, surely he could survive a failure. He then asked himself how the sea, stormy and terrible, sank all those ships, yet a little delicate shell could survive. Again the answer came to him, as answers do, not when he was thinking but later, in the warmth of his home, when he had forgotten all about the day's experiences. He realized that the ships battled and struggled against the waves and were wrecked, but the tiny shell *went with* the storms and waves and survived. That particular shell, incidentally, is known as the "Angel's Wing."

You must accept failure as a fact of life. It has all the power in it needed for success; recognize this fact. The tragedy is that when the person who has failed tries to start again and finds he can't, he says he needs capital, ideas or business premises. He does not realize the formula for success is neatly packaged in his failure.

If you analyze all your failures, you will find a reason or perhaps many reasons for each one. Success is found in failure, for there is a reason for each and every failure. Find the reason and you find success.

You can even double or triple your failure rate because failure has so much power in it. Don't make the mistake of thinking of failure as the enemy of success — it isn't. Failure is a teacher, a harsh one, but nevertheless it is the best one. You can be discouraged by failure or you can learn from it.

When Satan himself announced he was going out of business once and for all, he put all the tools of his trade up for sale. All his jars and vials stood in neat rows on long shelves, each bottle was labeled and priced. One jar was labeled Deceit, another Meanness, another Jealously; there were also Revenge, Envy and Greed, Dishonesty and Spite, Selfishness, Malice and Hatred. Everything was there, all the wiles and ruses of Satan. All marked up and ready for sale. However, one huge jar, larger than all the rest, but practically empty, had no price on it. Satan looked at it with a leer and said, "I don't even charge for that one, a tiny pinch of it and a man is mine; I can use him for any reason that suits my purpose and I do. The jar is nearly empty now, because I have used it on almost everyone, and the joke is that only Apprentice Millionaires know it belongs to me!" The label on the jar:

Discouragement

I repeat, you can be discouraged by failure, or you can learn from it, so go ahead and make mistakes. Make all you can, because remember, that's where you will find success: on the far side of failure.

When you get discouraged think of the words of Jacob Riis, "When nothing seems to help, I go and look at the stone cutter hammering away at a rock, perhaps a hundred times without so much as a crack showing in it. Yet at the hundred and first blow it will split in two and I know it was not that last blow that did it, but all that had gone before!" Keep on keeping on. Carry a little card around with you with these lines, by Charles Dickens, written on it:

Ride on! rough shod if need be, smooth shod if that will do, but ride on! Ride on over all obstacles, and win the race!

Florence Nightingale had a desperate struggle finding herself. She wrote in her diary, "In my 31st year I see nothing desirable but death." But she kept on and ultimately succeeded. Her work gained worldwide fame and recognition. She lived to the ripe old age of ninety. She is a household name and there are not many people in the Western world who do not know of her achievements. You have my assurance that no matter how much you have failed, no matter how despondent you have become, success is to be found on the other side of failure.

Some time ago, before the manuscript of this book was sent off to the publishers, a friend of mine, Paul Henry, called to see me. It was obvious to me that Paul was not making out the way he should and I let him read a copy of the rough draft manuscript, saying that I hoped it would help his plight, and if he had any constructive ideas or criticisms I would welcome them. The next day Paul returned the manuscript and when he did, he looked bright-eyed and full of enthusiasm despite the fact that he had stayed up all night reading it. He was impressed, he told me. But he went on even further and said, "Ron, I really did get an awful lot from your book, it has given me a new lease on life. If you really don't mind my criticism here are a few questions I would like to ask." He gave me a list, which read as follows:

1. You keep saying that if I just meditate in S.S.S. things will really happen. Is this really true?
2. I can see what you mean about visualizing every night and every morning but does it really work?
2. You keep mentioning the fact that the all powerful subconscious mind never makes a mistake, and it will give you brilliant ideas for success, but what I want to know is how can you tell if the idea is from the subconscious mind and not the conscious mind?
4. Last, but not least, you know I am really in the mire, and in the chapter "Power Failure" it's all very well to talk about frogs in bowls of cream, cockroaches, spiders' webs and Angel's Wings, but I am numbed by it all, my problems are for real.

Well, that is the lot, Ron, I hope you don't take offence.

Your indebted friend,
Paul

After I had read Paul's comments I realized I was indebted to him, for he had brought up some very valid points. We went through them one by one and this was the outcome of the ensuing conversation.

1. What you must understand is that what I am telling you has nothing to do with magic or witchcraft, it is only basic psychological principles used by super, super salesmen and top businessmen worldwide. Yes, to make things happen, Paul, the mind must have regular periods of quiet to enable you to hear the things the subconscious mind tells you.

2. Again, not by magic, but through psychological principles and as a result of visualizing, the subconscious mind knows your desires and starts to create a plan *"within your capabilities"* to enable you to attain your goals.
3. Ideas that come from the subconscious mind *feel* right. They come in the form of Eurekas! (I've discovered it!) You really do have a brain wave. Solutions to problems and ideas suddenly dawn on you and you *know* they are right because everything falls into place. When a Eureka! presents itself the idea is so right that you will never be able to find fault with it or pull it apart. The more meditation in S.S.S. you get and the more visualizing you do, the more enlightened you will become. So powerful is the subconscious mind you will soon see what I mean if you practice regularly.
4. Paul, after all is said and done, I think you should go back to the chapter on Action and read it again. I definitely hint that the secret of success is in the things we have not done and that everybody thinks and acts differently towards life. You see, because of the foregoing the secret for one man's success will be different from the secret of another man's success. One man may be persistent, but may have no faith. It is only when he discovers faith that he will find his secret of success. Another man may have faith but no sales ability. Only when he discovers how to sell does he discover his secret of success.

The power is in the things we have not done. If you have been in business and not made a fortune, or tried to achieve something more and have not, but at the same time you have not completely failed, this is your secret: *You have not tried hard enough. You have not risked everything on the turn of the wheel in order to win.* If, on the other hand, you have failed and not yet succeeded at all, you are almost there. Your secret is in the failure and in trying to discover where you went wrong, I wouldn't be tempted to examine other people too closely, only *yourself.*

I asked Paul what he thought the secret of success is. He had read a lot of inspirational and motivational books and the biographies of many of America's industrialists, salesmen, and financiers. I asked if he agreed that any of the following examples is, conclusively, THE secret of success. Henry Ford once said that the secret of his success was that when he had finished a job he had no reserves. By that he meant that he put everything into every job. A famous lion tamer once said, on being asked what the secret of success was, "A lion tamer must always be one move ahead of the lion, because if the time ever comes when the lion is one move ahead that will be the end of his days as a lion tamer." Perhaps the secret of success is keeping ahead of one's competitors and keeping on top of one's businesses.

The late George Caldough, of the *Business Ideas Letter* in London, wrote "Many people miss the central point that Napoleon Hill makes in his classic work, *Think and Grow Rich*. It is not the NEW ideas that make people rich, for there are very few truly new ideas. It is the adaption of one or more existing ideas to your own abilities and circumstances that will help create your future."

Paul still didn't appear to be satisfied and suddenly he said, "Well Ron, give me some specific examples of what you did in your life to overcome failure." Paul had caught me unawares and I blurted out the whole story.

"Paul, I knew that if I kept pushing myself beyond my capabilities I would ultimately fail, but I also knew that if I studied the failure I would discover the secrets of success. However, what I didn't realize was the pain and remorse that came with failure — the loneliness, embarrassment and humiliation I had somehow overlooked, but which all of a sudden had overwhelmed me.

"You must appreciate, Paul, that the failure I'm talking about was not one of my many initial failures where I had worked myself out of debt and built up businesses from nothing. The failure I'm talking about came when I was right at the top, flying high and sitting pretty. And believe me the higher you get the harder you fall! At the time I didn't realize that although there was plenty of room at the top of the ladder there was no room for sitting down!

"I'm the first one to tell you that if you habitually refuse to meet trouble head on you'll learn precious little so I'm not advocating running away from failure, but I'll tell you what I did in this instance. I put 3000 miles between me and my failures, my creditors and anyone else who could have wanted to label me finished.

"Then I had to realize that although I had been to the top, nobody owed me a living. In fact I had to start right at the bottom again, washing dishes, doing odd jobs, carpentry, you name it I did it, until I gradually built myself up again.

"You see when I failed I not only lost all my real estate, businesses, money, cars and possessions, but also my self-esteem, self-confidence, sales ability, wit, charm and personality. I wanted to hide under a rock, I couldn't face people, I couldn't deal or talk with people — therefore I couldn't sell.

"I figured the burden of failure was such a load to carry on one's shoulders that it could bog me down forever. I took heart from the fact that the majority of self-made millionaires had or have nearly been bankrupt at one time or the other and I reckoned that if I allowed failure to bog me down I would never be able to repay any of my debts, lead the good life again or achieve any more goals.

"I figured if I could hang on to my sanity I'd at least have my mind and my business acumen. To build up from nothing in a strange community seemed a better alternative than fighting creditors off in a place where everyone knew I was a failure.

"Milton made the understatement of a lifetime when he wrote 'The mind is its own place, and in itself can make a heaven of hell and a hell of heaven.' The biggest battle of all when you fail is with your own mind.

"Paul, it is difficult to hold your head high, meditate and generate new ideas when people are hounding you and ridiculing you for failing. The internal dialogue speeds up when you fail, the mind tape keeps repeating itself over and over of all the failures, the things you should have done, the things you should not have done. It is of the essence to stop the internal dialogue, and I found it beneficial to at least physically get away from my failures to enable me to recoup my losses."

Make more than a mental note that the antidotes to failure are all in this book and consist of visualizing your goals with faith and belief, S.S.S., stopping the internal dialogue and listening for and carrying out the Eurekas!

A strange phenomenon, called the cubic centimetre of chance, occurs when you fail. It probably happens at other times in your life, but it is when you fail that you are most able to recognize it. The cubic centimetre of chance happens when you are at your lowest ebb, absolutely down in the pits and you either meet someone who can help you or a fantastic opportunity occurs that would not have happened ordinarily.

All the most exciting, helpful and colourful people have come into my life just when I needed them. All the big opportunities of my life presented themselves when I was at rock bottom. The cubic centimetre of chance is not always obvious at the time, but, in retrospect, you can see that if you hadn't failed and been in that particular position you would not have met the particular person or been offered that certain opportunity. It would seem that the cubic centimetre of chance only puts in an appearance to those who *absolutely refuse* to give up no matter how adverse the conditions. Keep on keeping on. Adopt the attitude that "everything happens for the best" and the cubic centimetre of chance will present itself.

While battling with overwhelming tiredness, depression and frustration I used to come up with all sorts of schemes. Suicide crossed my mind more than once and, knowing what I know about the mind and brain, I even devised a special foolproof jig to enable me to fire a bullet through my head at the angle best ensured to do the job and not leave me a vegetable, as happens in so many attempted suicides.

Robbery and other illegal schemes went in and out of my mind and I must say that if I was that way inclined I'm sure I have a brilliant criminal mind. I came up with some brilliant schemes, so brilliant I dare not commit them to paper for fear someone might follow through on them.

Needless to say I neither committed suicide nor turned to crime. What I did do was keep on keeping on — no matter how tired, depressed or frustrated I was. Every day I would make sure I did just one little thing to help turn failure into success. It might have been reading a book, writing a letter or making a phone call. I used to write over and over again: "There is the ultimate knowledge to be gained that is *otherwise unobtainable* and *not available* to persons who have not failed." I was right!

You have to analyse failure and make it work, for failure can either be a stepping stone to success or a stumbling block to defeat.

Four-hundred years before Christ, Sophocles said, "There is no success without hardship." Seneca followed with, "Fire is the test of gold; adversity of strong men." And Emerson wrote, "Every calamity is a spur and a valuable hint." They were right!

ZOOM SECRETS!

1. When you fail you must look at that failure as the best thing that ever happened to you, and see how you can profit from it.
2. You will never get anywhere in life until you ''don't give a damn'' what people think of you. However, don't make the mistake of being over-aggressive, which is just as fatal to success as timidness.
3. If you have extravagant taste make sure you are paying for those extravagances out of profit, not merely out of cash flow. The sure-fire formula for failure: *spend more than you earn.*
4. You must make failure work for you. It is not without cause that most successful men find their great successes immediately after their greatest failure. Through analysis they discover the cause of their failures and in doing so discover the secrets of success.
5. The biggest battle of all, when you fail, is with your own mind. Take this book up into the hills with you and discover the antidotes to failure, which are S.S.S., stopping the internal dialogue, and visualizing.

CHAPTER 9

POWER CUT

*"I must stand with anybody that stands
right, stand with him while he is right,
and part with him when he goes wrong."*

ABRAHAM LINCOLN

You can greatly increase your personal power by having
a power cut. It makes little difference what your status
is at the present moment, because anyone, wherever
he is on the financial-social scale, can have a power
cut immeditately and without cost. You will breathe
freer, your load will be lightened, you will notice the
benefit overnight.

You instantly increase your personal power, first,
by cutting out of your life people who mentally and
physically exhaust you, as well as those who hold you
back in your search for wealth; secondly, by cutting
out bad habits that have become a very part of you;
and last, but by no means least, by cutting out unnecessary expenditures that financially drain you and
your resources — hence, the "power cut."

PEOPLE

Some people cling like big black rats, sucking the
very life blood out of you and your business. These
people come in many forms and guises: one may be
stifling your initiative, another suppressing your enthusiasm, another may perpetually let you down in one

way or the other. These people are so subtle they usually go unnoticed for years, until they cause you to suddenly drop dead from fatigue or nervous exhaustion.

If you feel anxious or depressed and care to analyse the situation thoroughly, you will find someone, somewhere, draining your energies unnecessarily. We as human beings were not made to run our lives for other people. We were made to do our own thing, what, how and when we please. It is only when we get caught unsuspectingly in someone else's web that things begin to go wrong. According to the Danish proverb, "He who builds to every man's advice will have a crooked house." Far too many people will give *gratis* advice, wish you to fall in with their lives and plans, and draw energy from you while giving nothing in return. These people drain you mentally. You will breathe freer the minute you cut these people out of your life. The Apprentice Millionaire has not got the time for them.

A very unsavoury task I face is asking you to examine your nearest and dearest friends. In this analysis you may find your best friend is perhaps your greatest enemy: he or she may be holding you back in your money-making endeavours. He or she most probably is not even conscious of the fact, but that person is holding you back, and neither you nor they may realize it. I will give you two examples: the first is of an attractive but grossly overweight woman. She was determined to be slim. She found it extremely difficult although she had more than her fair share of diet sheets and will power. The trouble was her husband. He would keep on giving her boxes of chocolates, wanting to wine and dine her and asking her to cook Italian cuisine, which they both loved. He didn't realize he was doing this, he just did it. You see, although they loved each other a great deal, the husband subconsciously did not want his wife to lose weight because he thought that when she was slim and attractive, she would "up and go."

Neither party realized the problem until I was asked to intervene. The husband's fears were quite unfounded and he is delighted with his "new slim wife." The other example is of the ultra-ambitious husband. His wife appeared, on the surface, to encourage him in all his endeavours to succeed. However she was, subconsciously, holding him back. Neither party realized what was happening, but the wife developed headaches, wanted to move to the West Coast, wanted to have a baby. All these things were in direct opposition to her husband's necessary requirements for success. Deep down she thought that once her husband had achieved fame and glory, she would be put on the shelf for a more glamorous model. As it happened, her fears were unfounded, because when her husband had made his pile, he was able to spend more time with her.

When we examine these examples, we immediately spot a few of the things that can help us to become star salesmen. The first is that we now understand that although our prospect may be really willing to buy from us, some third party may be subconsciously trying to stop the sale. Look at the first example again: the wife (call her the prospect) wanted to be slim; she had made her mind up, just as a prospect may make his mind up to buy from you. The husband (call him the third party) subconsciously didn't want her to lose weight. On the face of it he did want her to be slim. He at least *told* her he wanted her to be slim, but his subconscious actions proved otherwise. We also learn once again about the subconscious mind, the creative plan-building mind. Obviously, the husband kept telling his subconscious mind that he didn't want his wife to be slim, he was in fear of losing her. The subconscious mind went into action and directed him to buy his wife boxes of chocolates, wine and dine her and so on.

You must analyse your own particular case. Only you can determine who is helping you and who is hindering you. In a particular instance where you find that your wife or someone near and dear to you is working in opposition to you, you obviously don't cut them out; you alleviate the problem by confidently taking the matter into your own hands and doing your own thing. You don't tell the person involved of your suspicions because you would simply lose control of the situation. It is far easier to manoeuvre, motivate and manipulate people if they don't know you are doing it.

Be it husband, wife, in-laws, partners or just good friends, eliminate the source of any power loss by careful analysis of yourself and others, cut out the power loss and restore your potential personal power. It is of tremendous value to you to realize that people, although they may appear to encourage you in your particular endeavor, may actually be working in *direct opposition* to you *subconsciously.*

Generally speaking, most people get caught in ruts. These ruts may be caused by family and friends subconsciously working against you. Many people are scared of success, even the success of a loved one. They don't want to move to a bigger home, relocate, make new friends or pull up roots just because *you* want to move up the ladder of success. If you can recognize and understand these things, you will have fewer qualms about having a power cut. You will understand that you have allowed these people to greatly diminish your personal power.

Ever since Freud coined the term "libido," there has been a lot of speculation about how to transmute the sex drive into money making and other creative endeavours. But no one will ever convince me that the act of sex ever drains one of power. In fact if you care to study, as I have, the lives of many millionaires and successful people, you will discover that most were highly sexed. What you will also discover, though, is that successful people are careful about the chase. They do not waste too much time chasing the opposite sex, simply because it consumes a great deal of time. One also has to be careful about the number of partners one has, not because of the amount of time spent on sex, but because of the amount of time spent on entertaining and diversifying. You see, it is inevitable that if you have a number of different partners each one, generally speaking, has different interests. Therefore you are caught in an expensive and exhausting trap, having to entertain, go to different functions and various activities, all of which are bound to keep you away from your goals and drain you of your energies and resources.

Peter, who came to see me for consultation, told me that although he was a "social success" his business and personal goals were getting further and further away from him. It didn't take long to establish that his term "social success" meant that he had three glamorous girlfriends, all of whom he entertained lavishly and regularly. It took Peter very little time to "cut out" all his wayward ways and restore his power once we had analysed the situation.

Andrew Carnegie was renowned for one of his success principles known as the mastermind group. This embodied fifty specialists with whom he surrounded himself in order to have the necessary knowledge at hand to enable him to run his steel business efficiently. From time to time he found it necessary to replace members of his "Group." In fact over a period of time practically every member of which his alliance was originally composed had been cut out and replaced by some other person who could adapt himself more loyally and enthusiastically to Andrew Carnegie's needs. The psychology behind this is very simple. Men's minds grow and work at different rates. It will do you no good whatsoever to associate yourself with men whose minds cannot keep up with yours. It is inevitable that if you are visualizing and meditating in S.S.S. you will be streets ahead of your employees. It is necessary to do as Carnegie did if you do not want to be held back in your money-making endeavours.

However, don't surround yourself with "Yes" men. You need to surround yourself with high energy, positive doers. Cut out of your life the lackadaisical negative types; their negation can rub off on you only too easily.

You have learned a lot about the mind. You have seen that the subconscious mind creates plans for success, built on and around one's desires and mental images. You have seen how it operates like a computer and analyses and assimilates all your personal liabilities, assets and knowledge into a workable plan for the attainment of your goals. You will now be able to see something that is going to be of extraordinary importance to you, namely this: you must be a *leader* and not a *follower* to succeed in your endeavours. The reason is simple; it is of the essence that you follow your creative subconscious mind if you are to attain. The conscious mind is but an act. Therefore, if you are a follower, you are following somebody else's subconscious mind. To attain your goals you must be a leader by following your creative subconscious mind. When people follow you, as they will, they will be following you with their conscious minds. This has the utmost bearing on whether you will succeed or fail, become rich or poor, happy or unhappy. You cannot possibly be following your creative subconscious mind if you are a follower. They say that to become a leader is to rebel against what you are doing at the current time. No longer must you sit on the fence and let other people decide for you what you are going to do with your life. You must accept responsibility, and you not only can, but you can enjoy doing so.

HABITS

Of course you will not enjoy leading either yourself or others if you worry. Worry is the most destructive of all habits. Although it is fortunate that we know a lot about the habit, it is equally unfortunate that most people don't take time out to deal with it.

The habit of worry can be broken down into three components. The best way to explain these is to imagine a large tape playing on a tape recorder. One reel consists of past worries and the other reel consists of future worries. The tape can be and is played both ways, and where the tape goes through the pickup is what is happening in the mind now, at this precise moment in time. Let us examine each component and cure the habit of worry once and for all.

Past worries consist of the things that either happened or the things which we wanted to happen but didn't. We keep dragging up the past, the terrible things that happened to us or to our loved ones. We are constantly reminded of things we did to other people but shouldn't have done. We feel guilty, remorseful and wretched. The internal dialogue consists of the things we should have done to avert catastrophes and avoid hurt feelings, both our own and those of others. The thoughts keep reminding us of how we failed and how unhappy we are.

The last thing on earth to do is to try to suppress these thoughts and forget them. Don't do it. It is a fatal move to drive these past traumas underground. The secret of dealing with past worries is to air them in daylight. Get the burden off your chest.

If you feel that you owe someone an apology, the sooner you make it the better. On the other hand, if you feel that someone owes you an apology, confront them on the issue, try to get an apology by thoroughly airing the problem. You might have to write letters or go see people — whatever — but get it off your chest.

Psychologists believe that by far the best possible thing for a bereaved person to do is to cry. So many people suppress their feelings but, in doing so, bottle up negative energies that will come flooding out sooner or later, in some cases in years to come. People don't cry enough or show enough emotion or let off enough steam. The sanctioned practice is to bottle it up, keep a stiff upper lip, hide the emotion.

It is absolutely essential not to bury your emotions about past traumas and failures. Confront them openly even if they reduce you to tears. If necessary keep reliving the traumatic moment until the tape runs out. It will eventually. An interesting fact is that people bury their true emotions in the congnitive system they use the least. If you are a Visual, you should try to get all of the traumas and failures to come to the fore by using the auditory and kinesthetic systems that you rarely use. On the other hand, if you are a Kinesthetic, you should relive your traumatic moments both visually and auditorially. Whenever you have a past worry, use the systems you don't normally use and run that mind-tape loop out. It is the only way to stop past worries from bothering you.

The only people without future worries are in grave-yards. The solution to future worries is positive action to completely divert the course of the thing you are worrying about.

This book includes many suggestions about how to dramatically alter the course of your life so that you do exactly what you want to and achieve exactly what you desire. The ultimate solution to future problems is listening to the subconscious mind and following through with the things it tells you to do. Back this up with deciding what you want for goals, analysis with pen and paper, lateral thinking, action and all the ways and means of solving problems included in this book, and future worry is not even a problem. It becomes more like a game.

In our analogy of the tape recorder we had one reel that was past worry and one reel that was future worry. The tape can play either way, but, as the mind can only contain one thought at a time, it either has a past or a future worry going through at any given moment, that is the present worry. Of course the mind is like a drunken monkey and often swings from one thing to another. You may find yourself thinking of past and future worries in rapid succession. Both past and future worries have to be dealt with in the specific manner I have outlined. Sometimes, however, it is nice to be relieved of worry completely. The obvious way to do this is to stop the internal dialogue, for that is exactly what most of the thoughts that flow through one's mind are. Stop the internal dialogue and you've found relief from worry!

It would be impractical of me, and a sign of gullibility on your part, for me to tell you that you can cure the habit of worrying overnight. You must work on it. You must deal with past and future worries differently. You must keep emptying your mind, meditating in S.S.S. and reading this book up in the hills. Cutting out the habit of worry can increase your potential a thousandfold. I have always maintained that if one is going to worry about a million little things, let each little worry be a dollar bill!

To enable you to achieve personal power it is advisable to be as healthy as is possible. On that point, I am sure we all agree. However, the controversy arises on the things the experts tell us to "cut out" to achieve this health and power we are looking for.

If we were to place around a conference table twenty or thirty experts on any particular subject, be it theology, psychology, investment, medicine or baseball, the resulting debate would be far from harmonious. In actual fact, although our debaters are all experts on one particular subject, there would still be a lot of disagreement, controversy and bickering. However, as an Apprentice Millionaire, we are going to disregard the experts, let them carry on arguing and, as from now, we are going to do our own thing. We are the masters of our own destinies, and in order to make sure that we are going in the right direction we will constantly analyse ourselves and our environs.

In the case of cigarette smoking, we realize that the revenue generated for the government, advertising agents and the manufacturers is a good enough reason for some of these people to persuade us to keep on smoking, but it is personal power we are interested in, not generating wealth for others. In my many years of selling and experience in training salesmen, I have seen how sales can be lost by the cigarette smoker. I know for a fact that you can't *Talk and Grow Rich* with a mouth that smells like a gorilla's armpit. This is common sense. Many a sale has been lost by a salesman walking into a client's office, only to find an embarrassing situation arise because there were no ashtrays. This in itself may seem harmless enough, but when you examine the psycholgical implications of having to ask for an ashtray and having the prospect find one, you begin to realize that the concentration needed for a good "sell" has been broken. Another salesman I knew got into a client's car smoking a cigarette only to be told that the prospect hated the smell and would he mind throwing his cigarette out of the window. A works manager I knew had just given up smoking, and if a salesman arrived who was smoking, the manager would politely show him the door rather than risk talking to him and being tempted by the offer of a cigarette. The occasions that could be cited would fill a complete chapter, but it is the principle that I am hammering home.

Another aspect of cigarette smoking we have not mentioned is that of stamina. In all the life histories I have studied of great men I have come to the conclusion that they all had stamina. Now if you reckon that you can increase your stamina by even only a small percentage by cutting out smoking, consider it worthwhile. You, as a Student of Success, need all the health and stamina, breath and power you can get. It will not come down a small white tube, however hard you suck.

By far the most important aspect of smoking is the reduction of the oxygen supply it causes. Blood cells are drawn to carbon monoxide two hundred times more than they are to oxygen, but unfortunately it's the oxygen we desperately need.

In his *Journals,* Emerson wrote, "A man of no conversation should smoke." You have plenty to say when you *Talk and Grow Rich,* so I say, "A man of conversation should not smoke." Cut it out, restore the power, usable power.

One aspect of selling is being able to show your prospect how to be able to afford your products. After all, people only have so much money, they can't possibly buy everything. Bernice, who sold cosmetics, used to do exactly this. She would persuade her customers to quit smoking in the name of health and skin care, and then get them to spend the money they would have spent on cigarettes on perfume and makeup. Bernice would always lend them a copy of Ernest Caldwell's *How You Can Stop Smoking Permanently* to help them along. It's a handy example to remember when you are facing a prospect who might buy from you but doesn't have the funds. Show the prospect how to raise the money and he'll buy from you!

Another habit fatal to the Apprentice Millionaire's success is that of procrastination. Do not waste time putting off the things you must cut out of your life. The moment you have a power cut you will feel a load removed from your shoulders. The big grey cloud that constantly hangs over your head will disappear. If you put into action all the suggestions for the power cut immediately, the positive dramatic results will be so conclusive you will kill off the habit of procrastination, forever!

For every item manufactured, for every pastime devised, for every kind of foodstuff available, an expert somewhere shouts "Give it up, cut it out, it is bad for you." One of the principles this philosophy revolves around is "Know Thyself." You must analyse your daily intake of food, your pastimes, your friends, your activities. Only you can decide what is drawing power from you and what gives you power. The secret is not only to analyse, but to take measures to correct any power loss. Without the power cut all analysis is futile.

OVERHEADS

The original intention of many businesses, to sell a product or service for a nice juicy profit, frequently gets lost. All too often businesses turn into breeding grounds for bloodsuckers or holiday camps for the idle. It's sad to see profitable businesses turn into uncontrollable monsters which, instead of producing healthy profits, produce unhealthy problems.

All too often one's personal life turns into a nightmare simply because one gets bogged down with excessive expenditures.

The overhead power cut is exactly the same for businesses as it is for private individuals. In my years as a business consultant it was an enlightening experience for both my clients and myself to see just what could be done with an efficient power cut.

Every single overhead cost and expenditure would be listed in detail on a large sheet of paper (you must do the same). I would get my clients to put down weekly expenditures as well as items that only cropped up quarterly or annually. Time and time again one item would be forgotten. I used to get my clients to rack their brains to think of forgotten expenditures, and invariably they would come up with one or two hidden items.

Once the list was complete we would ruthlessly prune it to an absolute minimum. Only when this pruning was complete could my clients breathe freer and their businesses begin to prosper.

An old friend of mine had a huge peach tree in his

orchard which, in all the time he had it, the tree never bore any fruit. He decided to do something about it. What he did was cut away from it all the vines and ivy that were literally choking it to death. No sooner had he done that than the tree produced an abundance of peaches. You must cut out all the unnecessary expenditures that are literally choking your business and your life to death. The only way to do this is ruthlessly; there can be no half measures.

Despite pleas of embarrassment from my client the first thing we would try for was a rent reduction on his premises. Sometimes we'd get it, sometimes not. When we didn't we'd look for cheaper premises. In many cases subscriptions to magazines and clubs were cancelled. Many times the likes of window washers, gardeners and office cleaners were laid off. The work would be done by the very person who hired me as a consultant to save that extra wage. Equipment that was on lease or rental was sent back if it wasn't being used enough to pay its way. Cheaper ways were devised for doing things presently being done with rented equipment.

Crippling heating bills were reduced by employing efficient insulation. Telephone bills were cut dramatically by using pay phones or telephone locks so that the telephones could be used for incoming calls only. Ingenuity is the name of the game — *once* you have *recognized* the liability! Employees who weren't actually earning or productive were either laid off or somehow or other given work that would definitely generate a profit — or a least the amount of their wages.

All too often I hear that employees can't be laid off because they have become personal friends or that accounts can't be closed because they have been open for such a long time. You can't afford to have feelings of guilt, sentiment or embarrassment when you are having a power cut. For once in your life you must do what is right for yourself and your business.

In every money making operation it is necessary to have a regular power cut. Reduce waste, cut overheads, cut pilferage, cut overstaffing. Climb every ladder, open every door, take the whole business down to its nuts and bolts, leave no brick unturned, take nothing for granted. You may have to do all this yourself. It is hardly likely that an employee will point out to you that he isn't earning you a profit.

Multi-millionaire Jack Cohen was reputed to have said "I'm a nagger, all I do is find fault." Many millionaires and successful tycoons use this tactic in their businesses. They analyse their business until they find the weakest link. This might be a whole department in the operation, a section of a department, or it might be an old fashioned idea or method which the business has used since time immemorial. They move in on the weakest link and do everything that is necessary to make it the strongest link, the most efficient part of their organization. Then, they discover the next weakest link and work on that until *it* becomes the strongest link. This process is a continuing one, all the way through the business, until they end up again at that which was the original weakest link and the process begins again. This *modus operandi* is used throughout the whole organization: cash control, distribution, buying office, fleet maintenance, shop floor and retail outlets. The tighter the reins are pulled, the more power you gain.

J. Paul Getty was constantly looking for executives who, on their own initiative, were habitually looking for ways and means of cutting overheads and production costs, not only on the drilling sites of his oil operations, but in the refinery, the transportation, and in his offices, where he employed a minimal staff. Getty was more than aware that a single seemingly insignificant idea can save thousands, and sometimes millions, of dollars when operated throughout the business over a period of time.

An example of cost reduction is shown in the automobile industry, whereby if the manufacturer can reduce the production costs of each $14,000 auto by the seemingly insignificant amount of ten dollars, by the time the hundred thousandth car rolls off the production line the manufacturer has made an extra million dollars! In the automobile industry, the technicians constantly devise ways and means of doing things quicker and cheaper, trying at times to save, maybe, one per cent per operation or per item. This one per cent cut, spread over a number of items, can make a seemingly insignificant amount turn into millions of dollars. The Apprentice Millionaire recognizes the truth in the saying that "a penny saved is a penny earned!"

Without reservation, I can tell you that 90 per cent of the businesses in this country have in their employ too many non-productive workers. The relationship between the shop floor and managerial staff and office wallahs is totally, in Getty terms, "ludicrous."

I once heard a Portland stone quarry worker being interviewed. Here is what he said: "Thirty years ago we had three hundred and twenty quarry workers and four office staff, now we have four quarry men and three hundred and twenty office staff!" A case of too many supervisors and not enough workers. Farcical is the only word for it, but embarrassingly enough the situation is very easy to get into.

Now is the time to make sure you know and understand the difference between productive and non-productive labour. There is a big difference between the salesmen who are selling and generating money, and the wage clerks who are putting that money in the pay envelopes and not generating money. From the previous statement you may deduce why many a successful businessman has thousands of salesmen working for him on a commission only basis, but does most or all the non-productive work himself.

No Apprentice Millionaire can afford not to fully

acquaint himself with the book *Parkinson's Law*, written around the now-famous premise that work expands so as to fill the time available for its completion. This work, by C. Northcote Parkinson, shows that the time it takes to complete work (paperwork in particular) can be reduced by vast amounts.

Many leading corporations bring in outside "hatchet men" to prune superfluous staff. One German corporation became so efficiency conscious it cut its central office staff from 2,000 to 250.

You will do well to remember that every compromise you make on the points of power cut is made at the expense of a loss of personal power. You owe it to yourself to have a power cut. The bigger the cut, the more power to you!

ZOOM SECRETS!

1. Be constantly aware that people can suppress you subconsciously. Although someone may, on the surface, appear to help you, he may be working in direct opposition to you. Analyse your nearest and dearest to make sure they are not hindering your Apprenticeship.
2. To succeed you must follow your subconscious mind. That is why you must lead instead of follow, because if you are following you are doing so with your conscious mind, which has no power at all.
3. To get rid of past worry don't drive the trauma underground — play the tape until it runs out. Get it off your chest. To get rid of future worry, divert the course of the thing you are worrying about. To get rid of the worries in your mind at the present moment, stop the internal dialogue.
4. By reducing your overheads you will breathe freer overnight. Don't ever forget that a penny saved is a penny earned and that a seemingly insignificant penny cut can bring you millions by the end of the year.
5. When you are having a power cut don't let personal emotions cloud your money-making judgement. Feelings of guilt, sentiment or embarrassment must not enter into it. Have a power cut and do what is right for yourself and your business.

CHAPTER 10

THE POWER IN BOOKS

*"How many a man has dated a new era in
his life from the reading of a book."*

THOREAU

Writer's block nearly made this chapter a nonentity.
All the other chapters had been completed for some
time, but for some mysterious reason "The Power in
Books" kept being put off. Nothing came although at
the back of my cranium I knew it was there. Suddenly,
Eureka! I had it. Why the writer's block? Simple: all
up and coming entrepreneurs, salesmen and businessmen hate reading books. It is a sort of occupational
block. They would appear to be trying hard to excel,
but it is perhaps too hard, because they miss out on a
very important power tool. They are working and selling so hard that they don't leave time for reading. On
the other hand, if you go into any business library, you
will notice how crowded it is with *topflight* salesmen
and successful businessmen, researching new angles
on things, prices of shares and solutions to problems.
These topflight entrepreneurs have learned the power
in books.

The Apprentice Millionaire often makes the mistake
of not grasping the fact that there is an abundance of
knowledge of things already done, of things that can
be done and of things that are being done in books!

"The Power in Books" has to be read to be believed.

W. Clement Stone, founder of The Combined Insurance Company of America, believes in the power of books. In a single year he has given away 100,000 hardcover books and over one-million paperbacks to young people, employees, company stockholders, veterans' organizations, inmates of correctional institutions and to schools and hospitals.

John Henry Patterson, founder of the National Cash Register Company, started with a capital of only $6,500. His organization grew into the world's largest manufacturer of cash registers with a working capital of hundreds of millions of dollars. Patterson used books as part of his program to teach employees business facts and to inspire them. You, too, can not only inspire and motivate yourself, but your employees as well with the power in books!

The phenomenal growth of the Amway Corporation must surely be attributed to the emphasis put on reading motivational books and listening to inspiring tapes. On being sponsored into Amway, the most important thing you are told to do — next to using the products — is "read the books and listen to the tapes!" The growth of the successful Amway Corporation is not an accident.

Visualize in your mind's eye a picture of Abraham Lincoln sitting in a candlelit room next to a blazing log fire and reading, then realize that "Leaders are Readers." Abe Lincoln not only read, but absorbed. He was particularly noted for absorbing information. He would read a chapter, then contemplate what he had read.

Francis Bacon recognized the power in books and added his two cents worth: "Read not to contradict and confute, nor to believe and take for granted, but to weigh and consider." It is very important to weigh and consider. Don't forget that by doing just that with Napoleon Hill's *Think and Grow Rich* I discovered that great ideas come while *not thinking* and that the way to sell is by talking.

One fellow who shall remain nameless read through a hundred or more motivational and self-help books. He painstakingly read each sentence, one at a time, re-read the same sentence, thought about it carefully and when he was quite satisfied, crossed it out with a black ball-point. He did not underline, but crossed it out, obliterated it! Having done that he went on to the next sentence, and did the same thing. Eventually he finished the book. Literally finished it, for not one legible word was left. Every sentence, every word had been scored through with ink. After about the hundredth book had been destroyed I came by chance into contact with this indescribable specimen of tellurian impotency, and asked him what he thought he was doing. "Looking for the secret of success," replied that human turkey. I ask you how can you look for the secret of success in a single sentence? It simply cannot be reduced to one sentence. It can barely be reduced to a whole book! Believe me, I know. That's what I did here. So don't go through crossing out lines in search of a sentence that will guarantee success and nirvana. Digest the entire book. You then have to take the things in the books and apply them, you have to get into action and do them! Because everybody in the world is different, each person needs a different motivator, each prospect needs a different approach when you sell to him, therefore to know the different approaches, you have to read. Books are the elixir of life, books will show you all the answers, books will motivate you into action, but after that it is up to you to keep on, keeping on.

Many years ago I took a watch of mine into the jewellers to have it repaired. This particular watch was rather old and was of sentimental value more than anything else. When I collected it the watchmaker handed it back to me and charged me a few dollars.

Before I left the shop he gave me a few words of advice, especially for older watches, but which can be applied to any watch with a mainspring. "Wind it up first thing in the morning, not just before you retire for the night like most folks do." He carried on further to explain, "The reason being, if your watch goes through the day with a freshly wound spring it will be better able to withstand any little knocks and jolts, thereby keeping better time than a watch with a run-down spring." In a similar fashion, if we start the day with a freshly wound up mainspring, we too will be able to stand the strain of life and the little knocks and jolts. How can we do this? By reading a chapter of our favorite motivational book before we start the day. Cram your head with mental vitamins, leave no room for negative, destructive, non-creative, non-productive thoughts. Supercharge your subconscious mind!

One thing to always bear in mind is that even if you only learn one thing and one thing only from each book you read, you will progress in an astonishing manner. There is no such thing as non-profitable reading, simply because there is no way of telling when your subconscious mind will use the material. Several of the books I have purchased for a couple of dollars have returned over $100,000 each. This represents a percentage return that would have put a beatific smile even on J. Paul Getty's face.

You have probably noticed people who suddenly accelerate ahead in life. Nothing seems to stop them. They overcome all obstacles. Then suddenly they disappear without even a trace, they are finished, bankrupt, destitute, failed. What happens to these unfortunates is this. They originally get motivated somewhere along the line into favourable action, probably through books, or maybe through some other person's subconscious mind. They visualize goals, they read, and they progress. Unwittingly, however, because their businesses flourish and expand, these entrepreneurs spend more and more time negotiating, buying, selling and running their businesses in general. So much so, and it happens time after time, that the business eventually grinds to a halt because the businessman is suffering from exhaustion. Were these same people to reflect on how they got there in the first place, they would soon see that they still ought to be taking time out, meditating in S.S.S. listening to the subconscious mind, visualizing and reading motivational books. Even the fastest airplane or the most powerful engine needs constant refuelling or eventually it will stop working. We too, need constant refuelling. There is no such animal as a perpetual motion. Our refuelling consists of meditating, visualizing and reading.

As an avid reader of biographies and autobiographies I soon learned that many a great leader, orator, financier or industrialist was a rebel at school. Only when he or she learned the secret of self-education did they begin to rapidly excel. This stems from a power we mentioned earlier, enthusiasm. These rebels were not enthusiastic at school, but as soon as they were awakened to what they were really enthusiastic about, they could start reading, studying and learning.

You have missed a very important point if you think this book can be read like a novel. It has to be read with pen and paper at hand, so that every time a point is made or an example is given, you can underline it and jot down ways and means of applying the advice to your own particular circumstances. Take notes, jot down ideas, underline any passage or quote that favorably impresses you.

Establish the habit of underlining in red pen any paragraphs, quotes or anecdotes that may inspire or influence you. It helps a great deal to emphasize these motivational goodies, so that you can flip through the book and immediately find something to motivate you. Authors would prefer to see the pages of their books covered in red pen markings, with well-worn pages and a used look about them, than see them sitting on a bookcase gathering dust. You can even buy special felt tip markers made especially for emphasizing reading material. The well known brand is the Hi-Liter; it comes in many different colours and is a very handy pen for "hi-liting" any quotes or sentences that impress you.

Use this book as a tool. Do not stop reading the principles in this book. In fact, after the fourth reading your subconscious mind will have taken over, and you will not want to stop reading. Use this book as a talisman, take it everywhere you go. It will bring you fame and fortune, not through luck or magic, but through psychological law!

What the author has put in any particular book has probably taken him ten or fifteen years, or even perhaps a lifetime, to learn. You cannot possibly hope to absorb and comprehend all that knowledge in a single reading of one or two hours.

It might interest you to know that I read Napoleon Hill's *Think and Grow Rich* ninety-eight times before I understood its full significance. A further interesting point regarding Hill's book is that each of the thousands of people I tracked down and interviewed who had read it interpreted it differently!

Do not make the same mistake as many do when they begin their apprenticeship by thinking that all motivational material is the same. Some readers will stick to only one philosophy because they are in fear of anything else poisoning their minds. Don't make this mistake. Two books may be as different as chalk and cheese, but each carries in it something the other does not, each book has its own message.

If you were to attend any university in order to obtain a Ph.D. on any subject whatsoever, you would be expected to read between two and ten thousand books in order to grasp sufficient understanding and knowledge to pass your examinations. Apprentice Millionaires, however, think that they are exempt from academic reading. I would be the first to agree that business and selling acumen are gained by practical experience, but nevertheless reading about what other people have done enables you to cut many corners and take two or more steps at a time up the ladder of success. Furthermore, books give vast insight into how different people and businesses operate in different ways. The vast foundation of your business knowledge can be formed by reading what others have done, and what you read becomes your own.

Many experiments have been done with scholars who failed examinations for one reason or another. Under hypnosis these students would obtain remarkably high results, proving that everything they had read had been retained by one part of the mind or the other. This is exciting news for Apprentice Millionaires, for it means that although we may think we have forgotten what we read, really and truly it is all there for the subconscious mind to draw on when it needs to. AND IT DOES! It is valuable to realize that everything you read is food for thought and fuel for the subconscious mind. The more grist the subconscious mill has in it the more enlightening the Eurekas! it produces.

Many of us know that when the Scotsman Andrew Carnegie retired from active business, brought about by the selling of his steel interests, he was worth over a billion dollars. What the majority of folks do not know is that he attributed a large degree of his success to books. In fact, he was so impressed by books he donated funds to build free public libraries throughout the Western world. In his home town of Dunfermline, Scotland, one of the first of 2,800 libraries was built as a result of his generous donations.

By now, you are setting a certain amount of time aside every day, come what will, for practicing meditation and visualization, looking at the scrapbook you have containing the things you desire, and seeing them in your mind's eye. Additionally, you must set aside a period of time every day for reading. You must make time for a definite reading schedule. This is the first thing you must do to realize the power in books. Secondly, you must join your local library. If you do not belong to a library, join one today. If you don't know how to look up a title, locate a book, do the research or look up facts you require, ask the librarians — they are always helpful. Ask the librarian to let you look at the *Books in Print Subject Guide*. Look under the headings of Salesmanship, Psychology, Motivation, Success, Happiness, Meditation, or whatever particular field you wish to acquaint yourself with. If the library does not have a book you want, the librarian can sometimes get it from another library. Reading can be done very cheaply: there are free public libraries, secondhand bookstores, and cheap paperback editions of most books. Thirdly, you must spend a few dollars every week building up your own personal library.

I hope I have stimulated your interest in meditation, quietness, the mind and the non-thinking processes. There are many hundreds of books on meditation, many of which deserve at least a cursory skimming even if you are not going to read the whole book. Another important fact to bear in mind is that most of the books you will read have bibliographies, which are further reading lists. On no account can you ignore these. There is much to be gained from further reading in each direction.

Never be frightened of wasting money on motivational books or money-making material. On many occasions I have sent ten or twenty dollars off to various mail order companies for money-making ideas and books. Never consider such money wasted. You need as much of this kind of stuff as you can get hold of. Even if you can't use the material immediately, don't forget that your subconscious mind can and will use all the material it can get.

There is so much to read; it may pay you to invest in some books that teach "speed reading." These invaluable techniques were studied by people like John F. Kennedy and Franklin D. Roosevelt. They, too, saw the need to increase their reading rate because of the amount of power to be gained from books. In all probability there is even a speed reading course or seminar in your city, and for the profit that you will receive from reading books the price may be considered cheap, whatever it is! Check out your Yellow Pages now for the nearest course. Also check out your local library, there are many good books on speed reading available. Read as many of these as you can in order to find the technique that is best for you.

In your early days, books may be your best and only friends. Truthfully, early in my career, when things got really tough and I not only had financial problems to cope with, but emotional, spiritual and physical problems as well, books were my savior. That is how I came to read so many books on psychology and the human mind. I was determined to conquer it rather than have it conquer me! To quote Montesquieu, "I have never known any distress, that an hour's reading did not relieve."

In building up your personal library of motivational and psychology books do not forget to read everything available about your own particular vocation. There are literally hundreds of books available to enable you to expand your knowledge of whatever business you are in or would like to be in.

The way to increase your personal power is to resolve your problems. Do not forget the wealth of information available in books pertaining to every problem known to mankind. Reading as much as is conceivably possible about any problems you have will not only help you solve them directly, but will also give the subconscious mind material to compute with. Benjamin Franklin never read this book, yet it was he who said

"Reading makes a full man, meditation a profound man and discourse a clear man."

Do not suffer from tunnel vision in your reading habits. Profitable knowledge can be gained by reading about subjects related to your own vocation. Let me give you an example: when I got into debt, I not only read everything I could on getting out of debt, but everything related to it. I studied accountancy and business consulting as well as the legal aspects of debt. Because of the stress and pressures the debt problem produced, I studied psychology, which led me into studies of meditation and stopping the internal dialogue. All these studies furthered my research on where money-making ideas come from and how problems are solved.

By getting interested in related subjects you can expand your business in directions you may not normally have thought of. The man selling nuts may well find it profitable to sell nut crackers and nut bowls and perhaps even different lines of nuts.

This is exactly how J. Paul Getty operated his oil business. Getty was not only interested in drilling for oil, but in refining, piping, shipping, and retailing the stuff. And it can only benefit the person selling cosmetics to read how cars, insurance, computers and houses are sold.

From reading books on magic I discovered the value of velvet jackets, fine clothes, diamond rings, flowers, colors and lateral thinking. I urge you to read books about Al Koran, Houdini and John Mulholland. Magicians, more than anyone, realize the truth behind "It's not what you say, but what you convey that counts!" My main concern obviously is making money, but there is a pile of wealth in books that you would not normally consider motivational or money making. Magicians know how to put something across to people, and that's what selling is all about. Don't be a magician, be magic!

Biographies and autobiographies bring to light many of the secrets of success in life. It is easy to see that many people risk their lives and everything they have in order to attain their major objectives. Among these kinds of people are racing drivers, mountaineers, lone yachtsmen, deep sea divers, astronauts and test pilots. Read exciting and fascinating accounts of dangerous exploits, let your adrenalin bubble, be inspired and get out into the field and do these things for yourself.

BOOKS! BOOKS! BOOKS! READ! READ! READ! Forget the parties, theatre, bridge night, do some reading. Who knows, maybe you will be inspired to go on the greatest adventure of your life, perhaps by reading this book! Remember that those who won't read have no advantage over those who can't read.

Another field I suggest you explore is psychology. Two types of psychology books are availabe. One is classical psychology, including such authors as Jung, Freud and Pavlov. To save a lot of time you can skim through these books for bits and pieces of information that may interest you. Valuable knowledge can be gleaned by this skimming technique. The other type is what I call the "Mickey Mouse" psychology books. Generally they are filled with interesting facts about the mind-body-and-people, but all the painstaking and often boring research has been omitted. The current spate of "Mickey Mouse" psychology books includes all the "How-To" books, as well as self-help, sales improvement, motivational and inspirational books.

Make sure that you are not the John Doe who read every self-help and inspirational book available. He listened avidly to every motivational tape that was ever produced. Every weekend he would go to this seminar or that workshop. Every one of these ventures was undertaken and absorbed in good faith. Transcendental Meditation one week, "est" the next, followed by the Silva Mind Control Method and then the Relationships workshop. Nothing was missed, each course was completed, each tape carefully listened to, every book carefully read. What happened? *Nothing.* John Doe, although he participated in all of the above, merely lived through them; he didn't apply them to his own particular life.

Most learning takes place at a subconscious level. Through the practice of visualization and meditation, the subconscious mind will tie all your learning together to create profitable Eureka! experiences. But remember, you must *act* on the Eurekas! Never divorce yourself from the knowledge that as powerful as the subconscious mind is, it only impels. It does not compel. As with golf or skiing you don't become an expert just by reading about it. Reading is not an end in itself, it is a means to an end!

ZOOM SECRETS!

1. Read a chapter of your favorite motivational book before you start the day. This enables you to withstand the jolts and knocks of life.
2. Join a library today. This enables you to have vast amounts of valuable information available at your fingertips — free.
3. Set a certain amount of time aside each day for a definite reading schedule. Don't forget that everything you read is retained by one part of the mind or another, and there is no telling when the subconscious will draw on it.
4. Spend a few dollars every week to build your own library of sales, motivation, psychology, meditation and "Mickey Mouse" psychology books.
5. Underline anything in your own books that inspires or motivates you. This has two benefits. One, the underlining is a positive affirmation. Secondly, when you go through the book again you can immediately be lifted onto a higher plane.

CHAPTER 11

MAN POWER

*"To my mind the best investment a young
man starting out in business could possibly
make is to give all his time, all his
energies to work, just plain, hard work."*

CHARLES M. SCHWAB

Man power can be split into three categories: the work
you do yourself, the work your partners do and the
work of employees. Many would-be entrepreneurs do
not have capital, plans, ideas or business premises. The
one thing they do have, however, is something we are
all blessed with; that's ourselves. Believe it or not, "yourself"
can be your biggest asset in the accumulation of wealth,
and that's where we are going to take our first look at man
power.

MAN POWER — YOURSELF

You must understand that the creation of all earned
wealth is brought about by hard work done by someone, either by yourself or by people you inspire and
motivate into working for you. It was Art Linkletter
who wrote, "People find gold in fields, veins, riverbeds
and pockets. Whichever, it takes work to get it out."

For some reason only known to themselves the
authors of most success philosophies tend to shy away
from a secret of success and a fact of life: *there is no substitute
for hard work*.

Although I am the first one to encourage you to take time out to meditate and visualize, basically all that does is to produce the Eurekas!, the foolproof ideas you need for success. To bring these ideas to fruition some work must be done. Never lose sight of the fact that success is one percent inspiration (the Eureka!) and ninety-nine percent perspiration (the talking and selling). In England they say, "Ideas are such funny things, they never work unless you do." Or to quote an ancient proverb: "Toil is the sire of fame."

Human beings were made to work hard and regularly. This statement is borne out by the facts that you can't eat for eight hours a day; you can't make love for eight hours a day; and if you play for eight hours every day it won't be too long before you get very bored. Pleasure activities are highly pleasurable mostly because of the small amount of time we spend doing them.

Most of the work you do will be talking and selling — and never let anybody persuade you that that isn't hard work. On most occasions when I've spent five straight hours with clients in my consulting room, I've felt absolutely mentally and physically drained. Public speaking engagements tire me out just as much. And, if you think door-to-door selling is easy, try it yourself. The reason why the talking and selling exhausts me is that I put *everything* in to *every* sale.

The greatest advantage of you being your own man power is that it brings equal opportunity to everyone seeking riches. Even if you have little or no capital, if you are prepared to work hard, especially in the initial stages, success will be yours. Don't be frightened to get your hands dirty. Many deals require that work be done on them before they can be sold. One millionaire's son, on his father's death, received instead of the inheritance he was expecting a card with the following written on it: *accept a priceless gift — the joy of work*. The fact remains that somewhere along the line someone has to work hard. In fact, Andrew Carnegie's motto was "Anything in life worth having is worth working for!" You must adopt the attitude that "I'm only happy when I'm working!"

Many of your relatives and friends will be amazed at the rapidity with which you accumulate your wealth once you have started putting this success philosophy into action. When they see your big limousines, your huge summer home and your 60-foot yacht, they will tell you how lucky you are. When they do, you can reply, "Yes, isn't it funny, the harder I work the luckier I get!"

MAN POWER — PARTNERS

There are many reasons why money seekers get involved in partnerships. Sometimes a businessman will look for a partner who can inject needed capital into his business. Another businessman may want honest reliable help and a third may just need extra brainpower. As the gambler said, "Two heads are better than one," and he had the coin to prove it!

Realize that partnerships do not necessarily have to be a lifetime commitment. On many occasions the profit can be great in both knowledge and money with relatively short term partnerships.

I have been involved in many partnership deals, some profitable, others non-profitable. However, all of them increased my business acumen a thousandfold and my knowledge of working relationships and psychology a billionfold.

The first partnership agreement I had was with a number of retail businesses and, in my naive way, I got into all sorts of problems with cash flow, overstocking, underselling and, of course, personality conflicts with employees. Fortunately for me I got involved with a very astute businessman who was much older than I, and also much more experienced. Together we paid off creditors, reduced overheads, organized the staff and sold really hard. For his efforts I gave him 50 per cent of the business, which I still consider cheap, for if he had not come along as sure as night follows day I would have lost everything. The partnership was mutually beneficial. I got the experience of a much older businessman and retained 50 percent of my business. He got 50 per cent of a business and all he did was work hard and use his business acumen.

The next partnership involvement was when I was a business consultant. I was called into a business that sold bathrooms, showers and ceramic tiles. After the owner had seen me straighten out his business for him and make it profitable (for my standard fee, which wasn't cheap), he asked if I would like to become his partner. I accepted and that, too, was a mutually beneficial experience. I never injected any capital into the business, but worked hard and got 50 per cent of the profits. I have gotten into many businesses doing exactly the same thing.

This is the important thing; it's of no use whatsoever approaching a business owner and proposing that he give you 50 per cent of the profits and in return you will make his business expand and produce more profits. You have to prove yourself *first*.

The next partnership example was totally disastrous. I got involved with a "Mr. Swindler." Through my own negligence and trusting nature I failed to get the agreement in writing. Quite by accident I discovered that "Mr. Swindler" had actually signed an agreement giving my half of the business to someone else. To take legal proceedings in a case like this would have been throwing good money after bad because everyone else had the signed documents and I had nothing. When I say nothing, though, I mean nothing tangible. Although I was sour at the time, in retrospect I consider the vast amounts of profits that I have made by my mistakes and failures and I rub my hands with glee!

There is a lot of money and knowledge to be earned from partnerships. If we care to study the annals of business we soon discover the get-rich-quick scheme via the partnership route; witness Sears Roebuck, Montgomery Ward, and Marks and Spencer in England, to mention a few. When we dig even deeper still, we find men associating themselves with others in the capacity of advisors, functionaries or in the form of mastermind alliances, even if they appear on the surface as the monopolizer. Andrew Carnegie, Henry Ford, John D. Rockefeller and J. Paul Getty are but a handful.

How come, then, if this is the short cut to wealth, do so many partnerships fail? It is true that more friends are made and lost in business partnerships than all other friendships put together. The answer is a simple one: dynamic psychology or the lack of it. The failure between two partners rarely has anything to do with their business acumen or lack of it. It boils down to the lack of understanding about human nature. We all understand we must work in harmony if we are to achieve, but in most cases that is easier said than done. Everything goes all right in the first instance, then we get the gradual deterioration and then the eventual breakdown of the partnership. The solution comes in the package of a basic psychological formula that I call the Roy Rogers formula because it was the millionaire screen cowboy from whom I got it. He said this is how he made his marriage work. Each partner at the outset agrees to give 90 percent of himself and accept 10 percent from his partner. That is it, nothing more, nothing less. The outcome is perfect harmony, understanding and profit. This is known as the 90-10 formula and can be operated in any partnership, including marriage. It is absolutely essential both partners agree to it and understand it. This is the only way to combat the thoughts that are forever going through people's minds, e.g., "Why doesn't he work as hard as I do? Why doesn't he come up with any ideas? Why won't he see clients? Why does he always clear off for golf? Why doesn't he sell as much as I do? Why does . . . ?'' Well, one could go on forever.

People involved in the termination of a partnership all think that they are the only people on earth with these thoughts. Little do they realize that nearly everybody has these thoughts about everybody else! Lack of communication and the lack of understanding about human nature and the human mind are the reasons for deterioration and failure of a partnership. ''If only I had spoken up earlier'' think both partners, but they realize it too late. One of the main objectives of this book is to teach you how to be a sunflower rather than a wallflower.

If you have even the slightest doubt about any partnership arrangement, I suggest you get your partner to read this and the preceding paragraphs. He probably thinks similar things about you, and it is high time you got together and had a friendly talk. Put the onus on me and tell your partner I think he ought to read not only the bit about partnerships but the whole book. Not your copy, he can buy his own, and then we all benefit!

MAN POWER — EMPLOYEES

One of the shrewdest and finest men I knew told me ''If young men would learn about people instead of business, they could sell the world.'' You see, if you understood people they would all buy from you; they would all do as you asked of them.

As far as success secrets go, you have fared pretty well in what you have read so far, but what I am about to reveal to you now can either break you or make you: your success depends largely upon your knowledge of psychology, in your ability to choose and inspire men who understand psychology and use it in their efforts

196

to sell and inspire those under them. Read it through, study it, absorb it and, above all, use it.

When you have a Eureka! you must ally yourself with sufficient man power to bring the idea to fruition. One of the best ways to do that is through gentle persuasion. One of the greatest leaders that America ever had stated that secret of leadership in six words, as follows: "Kindness is more powerful than compulsion." Charles Schwab once said that to get the best from employees "Give praise lavishly." You must keep on giving praise lavishly if you are to get the most from your man power. Dave McIntyre knew this and said "Appreciation is like an insurance policy, it has to be renewed every now and then." The psychology behind that powerful truth is that everybody is interested in self-advancement, growth, a better and higher standard of living and freedom — they are not interested in being compelled to do things. The secret, then, is that employees must be able to *see* that by working for you, they can progress. They must be able to *see* the next rung of the ladder, they must be able to *see* wage increases, security, higher positions; they must be able to *see* potential.

Conversely, the consumer, the customer of your goods or services, must be able to *see* how and why your product or service will improve his world, his standard of living or his security.

In your studies as a Student of Success it will become overwhelmingly apparent that all the great industrialists, tycoons, financiers, statesmen, entrepreneurs and leaders all learned the secret of man power, the secret of dealing with men, in short, dynamic psychology. You want to be an Entrepreneur Par Excellence, well do you? YES! YES! YES! Then, learn about men, what they want and why!

All the great men realized that it is impossible to do everything themselves or to be in more than one place at a time. Dealing with man power is a secret that most men take a lifetime to learn, if they ever learn it at all. Man power has within it a power to close factories, demand wage increases, turn profit into loss overnight and vice versa. J. Paul Getty once faced a man power problem over a wage hike. He told the unions, against the advice of his labour relations experts, that the company could only afford to pay half what was being asked, but, Getty hastened to add, if production and profit kept up he would be willing to talk about the other half of the increase within the year. The unions agreed and the factory carried on working, without costly closures and strikes. Perhaps Getty had heard Churchill say, "Jaw, jaw, jaw, is better than war, war, war."

No matter how few or how many employees or customers you have, they are the heart of the business. Without them there is no business. That old undertaker knew what he was talking about when he said "Bodies is business." Unfortunately most employees are the type who would like a twenty-four hour week, not a forty-hour week. However, the kind of executive you are looking for is the man who tries to get forty hours into a twenty-four hour day. These are the people you want in key positions in your outfit. Once you have them, hang onto them. In the early days of your business your "whiz kids" may well earn in excess of what you do. Have no fears, this is the right way to do it. Give, give, give. *Then* take, take, take. But you must give first.

When I first started in business I intuitively gave, gave, gave to my employees; although at times it didn't seem right that many of them were better off than I was. It didn't seem good business sense that my employees were raking it in. It only dawned on me years later that the only reason I could build businesses of large proportions quickly was the fact that I gave, gave, gave to my employees. What brought it to my attention was observing many an entrepreneur trying to get projects off the ground in their initial stages and failing. They failed simply because they wanted their cake and to eat it, too, They wanted to build a business but at the same time they tried to retain all the profits, perks and benefits for themselves. To reiterate a very important point, to build a business, Give, Give, Give — then Take, Take, Take. But you must give first.

When I started out I used to be very disappointed with my man power; then I began to understand my own mind. What I discovered was that if I lowered my expectations of my man power, they would continually surprise me. Previously, I had always expected too much from my employees and never got it.

When you lower your expectations of your man power, don't forget to keep a sharp lookout for those who are continually exceeding your expectations. These are the people you want as executives, partners and advisors.

All is not how it would appear; men need more than money to be happy at their work. This you must understand: your man power must have job satisfaction. Many a man has left a highly paid, repetitious production line job for something more interesting, something more satisfying, maybe where he can see the end product of his labor rather than handle the same component and operation every day. He may earn considerably less doing this type of work but he has job satisfaction, something to live for; he is no longer an automaton doing soul destroying work.

Another instance of job satisfaction is the star salesman who takes the job as sales manager. In doing so, he might earn a lot less than when he was a salesman, but now he has control over men. Power, not money, brings his satisfaction. Your success is primarily dependent on the way in which you approach man power.

Status and symbols are both good ways of inspiring men to work. They are often cheaper than wage increases. The executive to whom you give a new title or larger office is bound to reward you handsomely with increased effort and production. You will do well to remember that power over men is in many instances more gratefully received than money.

During wars the suicide rate drops dramatically — this shows how the human mind works: although the scope for earning money is not there Man Power has an objective. In the case of war, the main objective is to beat the enemy and attain freedom. Even the man doing the most menial task can feel his importance in the war effort. He is doing his bit as it were, everybody is pulling together for a common cause. Everyone is everybody else's friend during the war, differences are forgotten. The major objective is to beat the enemy. If you can organize and motivate your man power so that they pull together for a common cause, the world will fall into your pocket.

No employee will work harder than you for long, and if you work in the same environs as your employees, be sure to set a good example. I will tell you what will happen if you have an employee who is working harder than you. It will not be long before he goes into business on his own. If you feel lackadaisical, unhappy or worried, be sure that you stay well away from your employees. Depression and indifference are just as contagious as enthusiasm and dynamism. Of course we know that to have wealth we must have action; we must build; create; do; achieve. All this can be done with the help of employees, with encouragement, harmony and incentive. Many an operation has been set up wherein the man power get the lion's share of the profits and the instigator gets one percent. This is how the one percenters make millions and the greedy apprentice fails to make the grade.

You must understand the psychology behind man power. Each man, no matter who he works for, still wants things — otherwise he would not bother to go to work, he would be a tramp instead. Remember that "Employees Want." Many a successful business has been built safely on this theme. Employees' wants not only incude money as an incentive but job satisfaction, holidays, plaques, mementos and books as encouragement. As John Locke pointed out, "Where there is no desire, there will be no industry." Other things employees want are good retirement, medical benefits and social activities. Evidence for this is the number of psychologists employed today by the larger corporations in an effort to smooth human relations. Businesses interested in their employees realize they should be given all the benefits they require and need. When successful, these efforts result in increased production, harmony and equilibrium.

Another success secret is the inspiring "pep talks" or inspirational speeches given by leading sales companies. These are given by all the biggest companies and organizations in the country and they really do keep up the morale of the employees. Many include singing and inspiring sales stories given by leading salesmen. Stir your man power into action with the spoken word in the same way as Churchill and Roosevelt did during the war. During the war, thousands of psychologists were employed on both sides to contrive demoralizing propaganda to deflate and undermine enemy troop morale. In times of peace we employ psychologists to contrive motivating, inspiring, enthusiastic and exciting things to induce people to positive, creative and productive action. Both work extremely well.

By far the item of greatest importance is realizing that every one of your employees has an internal dialogue going through his head. To find out what is going through the minds of your employees, put yourself in their place. Would you enjoy doing the job they are doing, for the pay they receive, in the conditions they have to work under? Be sensitive to their needs and feelings. For all you know an employee may hate you or the job he's doing unnecessarily. With a little foresight you might be able to change his attitude by making some small alteration in his conditions or environment.

Remember, also, that your employee's internal dialogue speeds up when he has only mediocre jobs to work on and also when he has personal problems. Although he may not say anything to you, his internal dialogue is with him all the time. It may be that he feels obliged to stay with you, or, on the other hand, he may already be looking for another job. He may tell you one thing, but be thinking another.

And, beyond all that, praise is cheaper than a pay raise. Too many rising entrepreneurs think they can cure all their man power ills with more money. Not only is that expensive, it usually doesn't work. We saw how some employees will take low paying jobs so they can see the end product and feel fulfilled. In the same way, your employees need praise, not more pay. They need to feel as though their work is important and appreciated. And praise is cheaper than pay.

All is overcome when you appreciate what he does and show that appreciation. Give praise lavishly!

ZOOM SECRETS!

1. Even if you have no capital, plans, or business premises, do not let this stop you from making money. All you need is "yourself" and you are in business. There is no substitute for hard work — and you will find that the harder you work the luckier you get.
2. There are many good reasons for going into partnership. Realize that partnerships don't have to be a lifetime commitment. You can make lots of profit in relatively short periods.
3. Make sure your partner has a copy of this book so that each of you understands the other's money making ways.
4. If both partners agree to give 90 percent and accept 10 percent, you will have discovered a way to run a successful, profitable partnership.
5. The best way to motivate employees: give praise lavishly!

CHAPTER 12

MONEY IS POWER

*"Money makes money, and the money
money makes, makes more money."*

BENJAMIN FRANKLIN

O.P.M.

Do you know of the party game where all the parti-
cipants sit in a large circle and the host whispers a
sentence in the ear of one of the guests? The sentence
is then passed around the circle in a gentle whisper.
Usually bits and pieces get added on or taken off and
gradually the sentence alters. When it reaches the last
guest, he or she has to stand up and say the sentence
out loud, usually to everybody's great amusement.
One sentence in such a game started as "I wouldn't
say life was lovely, but if I was a millionaire I wouldn't
be depressed." It ended up as "I wouldn't say my wife
was ugly, but if I was a builder I'd have her demol-
ished"!

I am convinced that if there ever were any secrets
about money, this is what has happened over the years
as the secrets were handed down from father to son,
from generation to generation. So many people appear
to have got it wrong; I will endeavour to square things
up again.

So far as borrowing seems to go, small thinking
has really crept in without subtlety. In a spirit of

throwing all caution to the winds, too much emphasis is put on O.P.M. (other people's money) — i.e., borrowing capital to start businesses and for expansion. It has become apparent that the entrepreneur has long forgotten how to generate money without incurring liabilities. Obviously, O.P.M. plays a big part in the great game of money making, but its secret has been handed down so many times the very essence of it has been lost. To borrow money to repay debts or to buy one's own private automobile and furniture is an absolute absurdity. It has been said the only reason why a great many American families do not own an elephant is because they have never been offered one for a dollar down and a dollar a week.

So much accent has been put on credit and O.P.M. that its true value to the entrepreneur has been lost long ago. You must understand that for this great tool, O.P.M., to work successfully, it must be used as it was originally intended. It is of no value to use O.P.M. on a scheme that is full of inefficiency and loopholes, where the overheads are too high and the profit margins too low. Using money as a substitute for brains and hard work is a common enough mistake. Before you borrow your copper cents, see if you can get by with common sense!

The world recession did not just happen. The only thing that can cure it is an increase in productivity, an increase in sales and a reduction in borrowing. The facts shown here are borne true by the fact that all over the world today, millions of people are grossly in debt to all sorts of money-lending institutions. Do not misconstrue what I am saying. My comments on O.P.M. are about how not to, rather than how to, do it. Millionaires like J. Paul Getty, Aristotle Onassis, and Walt Disney were heavy borrowers, but they borrowed for specific business purposes, not to pay off debts, buy cars or to purchase possessions. The magic of O.P.M.

will zoom you to wealth very quickly with minimum risk, provided you follow a few simple rules.

1. Make absolutely certain that what you require the loan for cannot be done without borrowing. Do not use money as a substitute for brains. Try to use energy instead of money.
2. Make sure you know exactly how the loan will be repaid, what the monthly payments will be and what the total amount of interest will be by the time the loan is paid off.
3. Do you know how, if your scheme fails, you will repay the debt and make a fresh start?
4. How much money will be taken from the venture itself after the loan instalment is paid? Will this be enough to live on and pay all other liabilities?

As a consultant of many years' standing I frequently hear "Knowing what I know now, I would not have borrowed the money in the first place." My clients follow up with queries about the likes of Henry Kaiser and Conrad Hilton, who borrowed thousands or even millions and apparently showed no concern towards the rates of interest they would pay, provided they got the required loan. When you have some real solid business experience behind you it is of course possible to make a profit from O.P.M. whatever the rate of interest, for all you are doing is playing with figures. So long as the scheme in which the loan is embodied generates more than the interest and capital payment and shows a profit, all is fine. Of course the big boys do an awful lot of homework on the figures, and, of course, they appreciate that the bigger the potential financial reward, the greater the risk.

I am a strict believer that if you really desire something, nothing can stop you from getting it. I give only a few guidelines on borrowing money. As far as I am concerned the borrowing is the easiest bit. The paying back is not so easy, as many a sad entrepreneur has found out.

The first rule is that you must operate with honesty and integrity at every level of your operation. You must realize that if you fail it is your solemn duty to repay every penny to every creditor, even if you do keep them waiting a year or two while you recoup your losses.

The second rule is to use the K.I.S.S. plan of action on every conceivable occasion: KEEP IT SIMPLE, STUPID. It's a standard research man's acronym which you will be well advised to remember. The renowned financier J. P. Morgan would not listen to a proposition that could not be grasped and understood in five minutes flat.

The third rule is that of having *alternatives*. Banks are in business to lend money to people — that is their major source of revenue. The bank manager is your friend, he is also the friend of the people whose money he has to lend you. In all fairness to his friends whose money he has the power to lend, he has to be sure, or reasonably sure, that you are a fair risk. It is doubtful that if one bank refuses you a loan another one will not refuse you unless you alter more than just your story and presentation. Although cash flow projections and personality count, the bank or lender will be more interested in your own personal track record and, above all, what collateral you can offer.

By taking out small loans and paying them back quickly, then taking out a slightly larger loan and re-paying that back, one can build up a good credit rating fairly quickly. The Apprentice Millionaire in a hurry can borrow a number of small sums from friends, relatives, brokers, mail order firms and use that money as collateral on a larger loan. If your house has sufficient equity in it, a first or even second mortgage might be the way for you to obtain a loan to enable you to zoom to wealth.

Another way around the O.P.M. problem is this: instead of going after money go after goods which can be obtained on credit. Sell the goods and use the money for whatever purposes you desire. You can build a business of enormous proportions using this technique as long as you are aware of the pitfalls and nothing goes wrong.

First, you must be able to convert the goods into cash. Second, you must have available cash flow to be able to pay for the stock within the usual 30 or 90 day credit period. It's very easy to get lulled into a false sense of security by large volumes of cash flow. Bear this in mind because it's particularly inviting to reduce the price of the stock to less than what it actually costs in order to create cash flow. The theory of this is fine, except that when things go wrong and the stock fails to sell, you can't come up with sufficient funds to pay for the previous month's stock, and the supplier then refuses to deliver fresh stock. The day of reckoning has arrived, and because you have been selling at less than cost, you have a shortfall in finances — what we in business term a LOSS!

A very valid point about interest on borrowed money: do you remember I mentioned in "The Secret of Goals" that if you had $40,000 invested at only 7 percent per annum, in fifty years you would be a millionaire? Well, don't forget the formula works in reverse, and if you are not careful about how you borrow, you can find yourself paying interest only and not getting any nearer towards paying back the principal.

An interesting final note: in my early business days I spent hours plotting and planning ways and means of raising O.P.M., with, to be sure, a large degree of success. I used to spend hours on the telephone with bankers, brokers and lenders, and even more time going to their offices for the appointments that I had made. The interesting thing is that when I had learned a lot about business I concentrated more and more on making money, big money, without O.P.M. or any kind of capital investment whatsoever.

DEVELOPING THE MILLIONAIRE MENTALITY

The best way to develop the millionaire mentality is to overwhelm your subconscious mind with the desire for money. There are many things you must do to tap, tap, tap, this message into the subconscious before it comes flooding out, heaped up, pressed down and running over.

First you must have a hip pocket roll. If as I suspect you don't have four or five hundred dollars to keep in a great bulging wedge in your pocket you must make one. Cut out paper "ones" and encase them with a couple of very large notes. If you can't afford a couple of big ones, small notes will do. Put a band around your hip pocket roll if you haven't yet been able to get yourself a gold money clip. I had my gold money clip made in the shape of the dollar sign. It creates the right impression. Stuff your hip pocket roll in your pocket, let it be seen, fondle it, tap, tap, tap the subconscious mind.

Whenever you part with your money never "kiss" it goodbye, always bless it and ask it to return to you a thousandfold. Develop positive attitudes toward money.

Whenever a tramp asks you for money always give him twice what he asks for. When you consider that in the course of a year you might be asked for alms about six times and, usually, it's a quarter they ask for, you'll give them 50 cents — and that's a three dollar investment over the course of a year. Money is made round to go round! Tap, tap, tap the subconscious mind. Show the subconscious how big you think in terms of money. Don't be small-minded. What you withhold diminishes, what you give increases. As Henry Ford said, "Money is like an arm or a leg, you either use it or lose it."

Change coins into dollar bills as soon as you have enough. Never collect small change — this shows your mentality, and that's all your subconscious will attract. Only collect notes — collect a million of them!

Always make shopkeepers change dollar bills for you, never fumble for the exact change. Deal only in big denominations. Don't be petty with money.

Form a large note into the shape of a three cornered triangle and carefully tape the joint. Never spend this bill. Just leave it by your bedside table where you will see it every night and every morning. The triangle represents the Trinity and symbolizes something without beginning and without end.

Flood your subconscious mind with the desire for money by putting dollar signs everywhere. When you open the refrigerator door what do you see, pasted on the inside? Dollar signs — hundreds of them! Draw a sheet of them out and put them under the alarm clock as a constant reminder, and put another sheet under your pillow just for good measure. Carry a sheet of dollar signs in each pocket and in your wallet. Keep looking at them, let the desire for money soak deep into your subconscious mind. If you are getting the impression that everywhere you look you'll see dollar signs, you are right, but you have only just started!

When you see dollar signs everywhere you go, you can say that you are on the right track. Now don't forget, this is important. Although you may consciously think it's silly and not helping you, don't forget that the subconscious mind, which is the most important, needs the repetition of mental images. It can't help but pick up on these dollar signs and start creating Eurekas! for the attainment of wealth.

Create an impression of wealth wherever you go. Don't get involved in trivial conversation about how bad things are, or about how little money there is to go around. Buy a jacket with a velvet collar, wear a flower in your buttonhole, buy a gold ring or a gold plated ring until you can afford the real thing. Be a showman, but not a showoff! All these little things create the impression of wealth and tap, tap, tap the subconscious. You will find you attract different people, new circumstances and profitable situations.

DEBTS

I love the story of the patient pouring his heart out on the psychiatrist's couch: "I have a luxury apartment in New York, a condominium, a Cadillac and a Corvette Stingray, a pretty wife, a mistress and a forty-foot yacht." "Well, what on earth is the problem then?" asked the psychiatrist. "I only make fifty dollars a week," replied the patient.

I also love the story of the farmer who was on the verge of bankruptcy. The largest single creditor, a bank, was owed a fortune. The bank manager, in a final effort to come out clean, personally telephoned the farmer and said, "I'd like you to come into my office and see me — you now owe us $500,000." The farmer replied, "If it's as much as that, *you* better come and see *me!*"

The foregoing stories illustrate the humorous side of the debt situation, but, believe me, on the whole, it isn't funny at all.

I can recall clearly the first night that it dawned on me that I had a serious debt problem. I was out in the woods strolling with my dog. The dog chased and caught a rabbit; he then proceeded to eat it, fur, head, legs and all. I felt the tears welling up in my eyes, and before I could stop myself I was crying like a baby. What I had found was a release for my emotions. (I'd seen my dog catch and eat rabbits before, but it had not had any effect on me.) This was on the same evening that my immaculate Trans-Am had been repossessed. The time was around 1972, when they hadn't been out all that long and were real eyecatchers. This one had the big 455 High Output engine, and I had RON HOLLAND IS MOTORCYCLES emblazoned down both sides. The sign writing was done in the same blue as the large firebird decal on the hood and picked out in grey, which made a real contrast against the white body work.

It was only in the woods that it dawned on me that I had real problems. I knew the car episode was just a start. Will Rogers wrote in his autobiography, "It is not politics that is worrying this country; it is the second payment." It is facts like the foregoing that prompted Abraham Lincoln to say "You cannot keep out of trouble by spending more than you earn."

Should you find yourself in debt, don't panic. There is always a way out, other than suicide. No, I am not joking. Any psychiatrist will tell you that men are more likely to commit suicide because of debt than for any other reason. Debt is a killer of all initiative, happiness, drive and reason and it dulls the edge of husbandry. Many a man would rather face active service sitting in a trench surrounded on all sides by the enemy than be in debt.

Unfortunately, being in debt is one of the most likely positions the Apprentice Millionaire can find himself in. Working your way out of debt will undoubtedly increase your business acumen a thousandfold. However, it's not good for the ego and you will do well to remember that many, many self-made millionaires have been either bankrupt or on the verge of bankruptcy. The key to success in any debt situation is not really a question of how to get out of debt, pay back the debts, or anything else. The issue is much bigger. It's a case of getting bogged down, giving up, throwing in the towel, becoming an alcoholic. Don't quit. Don't get bogged down. Don't give up. Do anything rather than quit! Take this book into the quiet hills, get some solitude, stop the internal dialogue, listen to the subconscious mind.

Thomas Carlyle spells out exactly what you must do in order to get out of debt: "There are but two ways of paying debts; increase industry in raising income, increase thrift in paying out.'' Now you need not think because those words were written many years ago that they do not apply today. They do.

Business principles have not altered one iota since the first flint ax was bartered by prehistoric man for two teradactyl eggs. Of course you can go bankrupt, and with a little bit of luck and a fair wind start all over again, but you will have learned precious little. By working your way out of debt you stand to gain far more business acumen than from all the other parts of your apprenticeship put together.

It is to no avail increasing industry in the raising of income if the CAUSE of the debts still remains. That can be likened to bailing a leaking boat of its water without blocking up the hole where it is coming in. No, you must analyse the situation. Are your overheads too high? Did you spend the money on too much advertising that did not pay? Undoubtedly your profit margin is not high enough. Have you been paying a nonproductive work force? Have you been taking too large a salary? It is up to you, and you alone, to find the cause. Once the cause has been found and, hopefully, remedied, you must carefully make a list of the creditors. Here is where the talking comes in. Go and see them personally and make arrangements for paying them back at 10 percent of the gross debt every month. Make it known that you wish to continue trading with them on a cash basis. In this way they do not lose. They are getting what is owed to them, plus they retain a cash customer. Communication is the secret here, and many an entrepreneur's downfall has been that he is too scared to go and see his creditors. In making deals like this beware that your overall monthly commitment does not exceed the income you have. If you have any debtors, go and see them. Arrange that they pay you back any outstanding monies at 20 percent per month. That's business! Treat each debtor and creditor as you would a favourite customer. "Plans get you into things," wrote Will Rogers, "but you have to work your way out." Let us review the scheme that is a foolproof way of working yourself out of debt.

1. Stop buying on credit, reduce all expenditures to a minimum — overheads, salaries, wages, advertising, etc.
2. Make arrangements by actually seeing the creditors and offer to pay them 10 per cent per month of the debt you owe them.
3. Make arrangements by actually seeing your debtors and get them to pay you back at 20 per cent per month.
4. Increase the business in every possible way, primarily by working harder yourself. The salesman training schools have a lovely saying for "old in the tooth" salesmen not doing so well: "Work and live for a year as you did when you first started selling."
5. Steer clear of borrowed money to pay debts. How illogical can millions of people get? What appears to be the easy way out will prove to be the fool's way in, much deeper in!

The way I see it, there are many ways around the debt situation. It all depends on what you want out of it. I suggest you use the foregoing method if you want to learn about people and gain valuable business acumen. However, there are other options available. You can, for instance, go legally bankrupt; many self-made millionaires have done so. You can disappear, become inaccessible and destroy your personal history, the way I did, and emerge only when you are really on top of the situation, as I did!

The most important point is this: whichever option you choose make sure you are in control of the situation. Either the dog will wag the tail or the tail will wag the dog. Make sure *you* do the wagging!

Here are a few notes I want to finish on. When I was absolutely cleaned out I literally didn't have enough money left for food. Can you imagine being at the top of the ladder one day and being at the bottom the next? One embarrassing incident, which I find rather funny now, was when I waited patiently in a pizza house for someone to leave a portion of pizza on his plate. At last, one guy left some pizza on his plate and got up and left. I immediately appropriated his seat and his pizza. No sooner had I taken the first ravenous mouthful than the guy came back to retrieve his briefcase, inadvertently left under the table. We were both equally embarrassed!

The final note, a happy one, is that one of my cars now is a white Rolls Royce with RON HOLLAND IS MOTIVATION emblazoned down both sides. Furthermore, I can assure you that now, nobody is in a position to take it away from me!

SPENDING

All I had intended to say on this subject is that millionaires don't spend and leave it at that, but I feel a few more words might be in order.

Just think of J. Paul Getty's pay phone in the hall of Sutton Place for the use of guests and Jimmy Savile putting one of his properties up for sale to enable him to get a free appraisal on it. It is equally hard to believe that John Bloom used to spend his pocket money on fireworks as a kid; when the stores ran out he would sell them to his school chums for twice the price. It is practically impossible to believe that Aristotle Onassis used to rent out his own room at night and sleep in it himself for just a few hours during the day.

The millionaire has one thing on his mind all the time. He has developed the millionaire mentality, he is loath to spend money on anything that cannot be converted back into cash, that cannot be sold for a profit, and that is not appreciating. He shouts at his buyers and sellers: "When you are buying the price is too high, when you are selling the price is too low, and you are not selling enough!"

The Apprentice Millionaire understands only too well that he has to speculate to accumulate. When he does he realizes the risks involved. This was admirably illustrated when J. Paul Getty bought up oil stock as fast as he could as the stock exchange collapsed, despite the advice of many eminent businessmen. They argued, "The business situation can only get worse." Many were adamant: "The economy will disintegrate completely." Well, Getty kept spending his money as he thought he ought and the rest is history. When you discover the significance of that last sentence, stop for a moment, light a candle and pour the wine, for the understanding of this one statement will be the turning point of your career. Write it down and study it: *HE DID WHAT HE THOUGHT OUGHT TO BE DONE.* This one sentence carries more in it, more wisdom, more of every conceivable positive attitude there could be than any other. The whole of this philosophy revolves around it, the doing of your own thing. Men will win or lose, sink or swim; all depends on whether or not they do their own thing, and follow their own subconscious minds.

On many occasions I have been criticized for using the likes of Hughes, Rockefeller or Getty in my examples. Those criticizing say, "But Hughes was left millions to start with" or perhaps another will say "But Getty was in the oil business in the boom period." Similar lines are used by the Apprentice who has to start with little or nothing, is not in the oil business and has no hope of getting into the oil business.

The reason for using the likes of Getty, Rockefeller and Hughes has a lot to do with their understanding of psychology in the dealing with men and a lot to do with their understanding of the secrets of money. As a poverty stricken Apprentice or even one who is halfway up the ladder it is very difficult to see the way that money can turn around and destroy you when it comes. It is very difficult to realize that once it does come, as it will, it is very hard to hang on to. The Gettys, Vanderbilts and Rockefellers understood that the secret of money is to invest it to enable others to earn a living by creating factories and jobs, or so that others may enjoy themselves by creating libraries and museums. If you do not control your wealth in a Getty type fashion, employing it for the benefit of mankind, it will destroy you in a much shorter period of time than it took you to generate and accumulate it.

SAVING

The serious Apprentice Millionaire cannot afford to ignore any of the great money-making secrets. The secret of saving has many benefits. When Byron wrote "Ready money is Aladdin's lamp" this is what he meant: to a Student of Success who has saved, many opportunities present themselves. The Student who can get in on the ground floor, can clean up, whereas the spendthrift will be chasing around for sponsors and people to lend him money. The fact that you have money behind you gives you great bargaining power; you need not sell your wares, services or ideas to the first bidder. If you want some shock treatment, calculate the best you can to the nearest thousand dollars all the money that has passed through your own hands in your lifetime. You will be amazed and shocked if you have not been systematic in your saving habits. J. P. Morgan once said that he would rather lend a million dollars to a man of sound character, who had formed the habit of saving, than he would a thousand dollars to a man without character who was a spendthrift.

The Student of Success who makes it a regular habit to save a proportion of his salary or business profits has more than a head start on the spendthrift. Bite the bullet now and put away 10 percent of your gross, the fun comes later, *and what fun!* You must adopt the attitude that money is a *tool to be used, not abused.*

Many a tycoon has made a million dollars, but on the grand day of reckoning, ended up without a cent. The money was just goosed away. Had saving and investment been part of the overall scheme the picture painted would have been totally different.

By saving, and investing your savings, you are playing both ends of the money making game against the middle. The rule is, you win every time.

The saving of money is solely a matter of habit, and it has not escaped my attention that the successful Apprentice Millionaire will stop at nothing to ensure that he does not break his habit. For argument's sake, he decides to set aside $20 every week for the sole purpose of saving it. Unfortunately his car needs some extra expenditure that had not been foreseen. The serious Student will automatically forego an evening out, cigarettes or give up some personal leisure activity to enable him to continue with his systematic habit of saving. An inner sense tells him that to break his habit of saving is going to cost him a lot more than would appear on the surface. He knows that with capital, collateral or savings behind him he is going to be ready when his golden opportunity rears its tantalizing head.

The whole function of saving is to have sufficient funds for opportunities as they arise. Many an entrepreneur will not bother to be systematic in his saving habits because he believes that "When the money begins to come in, it comes flooding in from all quarters and with so much ease you wonder where it has been when things have been so thin on the ground." This is true in itself; when the money does come, it comes big, but to arrive at this desirable state of affairs, many deals, much learning and many opportunities have to be grasped. It is so much easier with savings behind you. As an old Yiddish proverb says, "With money in your bank, you are wise, you are handsome, and you sing well too.''

ZOOM SECRETS!

1. Make sure that what you require a loan for cannot be done without borrowing. Try to use energy instead of money.
2. When borrowing money the lending institutions are more interested in your collateral than in anything else.
3. Flood your subconscious mind with the desire for money. Make a hip pocket roll out of paper and encase it with a few dollar bills. Bless your money when you part with it and ask it to return a thousandfold. Don't collect small change, it shows your small change mentality. Collect only large notes — collect a million of them. Put sheets of dollar signs where you will be bound to see them. Saturate the subconscious and await the Eurekas! that will show you how to attain wealth.
4. In a debt situation, although there are many options, make sure that with whichever one you choose, you are in control. Never forget that either the dog wags the tail or the tail will wag the dog. Make sure *you* do the wagging!
5. When spending money make sure that what you buy appreciates in value and can be converted back into cash.
6. Cultivate the habit of saving so that you have enough funds to get you in on the ground floor of any opportunities that should arise.

CHAPTER 13

KNOWLEDGE IS POWER

"Knowledge is power."

FRANCIS BACON

The modern Apprentice Millionaire needs his pile now, as soon as conceivably possible, so that he may enjoy the fruits of his labours while he is still able to. Long gone is the "pie in the sky, by and by, when you die" attitude. The modern attitude is: I want my pie now, down on the ground while I'm still around — with ice cream on top!

Not only is the attitude understandable, but I wholeheartedly endorse it. To enable us to zoom to wealth it is necessary to grasp as many success secrets and psychological tools as possible. Because human beings are individuals, everybody thinks and acts differently towards life. This means not only that your prospects need approaching in different ways, but you as an individual will have to decide which route to take towards your many goals. As the German philosopher Nietzsche put it, "This is my way; what is your way? *The* way doesn't exist."

One truth that does remain constant for all and sundry people are Francis Bacon's words, "Knowledge is power." Too many times I have heard his statement contradicted. Francis Bacon got it right first time around, knowledge *is* power.

I will endeavour to explain. Who was Francis Bacon? Well, apart from being a scientist, writer, philosopher and Lord Chancellor of England he was a Rosicrucian. You ask, is that significant? I think it is. My research has led me on all sorts of adventures and in my quest for the truth about the mind and man's quest for riches I have made many discoveries. The Rosicrucians' whole way of life for thousands of years has revolved around meditation, visualization and the power of the subconscious mind. Many of the things we have been discussing in this book.

Knowledge is power only when you know why. The reason why knowledge is power is the simple fact that: *the more knowledge your subconscious mind has to draw on the more illuminating Eurekas! it will create for you.*

PSYCHOLOGICAL KNOWLEDGE

By far the most important bit of psychological knowledge you have acquired so far is that it is vitally important to stop the internal dialogue to enable you to hear the Eurekas! from the subconscious mind.

I don't usually take Emerson to task, but as far as the following quote goes I will, Said Emerson, "What is the hardest task in the world? To think!" Well, that's definitely wrong. What is the hardest task in the world? Not to think! Right! You can prove it to yourself simply by thinking about it. That's relatively easy. Now try to not think about it. It won't go away, will it? You can't not think about it until you learn how to stop the internal dialogue.

We must meditate in S.S.S. Plenty of Silence, Stillness, and Solitude is the key to the mind. We have already discussed staring at a candle flame a single minute at a time with the aid of a digital clock. What must be remembered is that although you may not seem to be getting anywhere with your efforts to stop the internal dialogue, every little bit helps, and the sheer fact that you are practising not thinking gives you a much better chance to hear the Eurekas! than when you are trying to sort your problems out consciously.

One method of stopping the internal dialogue is the use of a mantra. A popular mantra is OM. All you do is repeat the mantra until it dies out, like this: "O m m m," then repeat it again. The mind can only carry one thought at a time and it is much better to have "O m m m" going through it than your internal dialogue. When you have stopped the internal dialogue you can stop using the mantra. You just listen, then, to what your subconscious has to tell you.

Another method of stopping the internal dialogue is just to stare blankly at a pile of leaves. Leonardo da Vinci used a pile of ashes which he stared at with resounding success. Something I use for staring at is a bunch of flowers. Flowers are fifth dimensional and lift you onto the plane of abundance with remarkable rapidity. I suggest you always keep a bunch of beautiful flowers in your retreat specifically for the purpose of meditating on. When you are staring at your pile of ashes or leaves or your bunch of flowers, imagine that you are emptying your mind into them, just stare blankly at them. Should a tear roll down your cheek just ignore it — this is a common occurrence. The important thing is to reduce the number of thoughts that go through your mind.

If you can get your solitude by going into the hills or desert that's fine. One of the best ways of stopping the internal dialogue is to walk fairly briskly, looking all the time straight ahead towards the horizon. Sometimes it helps to slightly cross the eyes. Always keep the horizon in view, but at the same time, try to get as large a peripheral view as possible without actually turning your head from side to side. In all these cases the S.S.S. will be doing you a power of good.

ESOTERIC KNOWLEDGE

Thousands, probably millions, of people are searching for answers, truths and solutions to problems in this fast space-age world we live in. In my search for the secrets of success, I tried just about everything out of necessity. I even tried numerology, astrology, tarot, this one, that one and the other one. And do you know something, they all work!

I would never dream of putting down any esoteric practice, but what I will say is that the psychological knowledge presented in this book is far easier to grasp and work with than astrology or whatever.

Without being contradictory, we have used S.S.S. and turned Zen into Yen, but everything that was taken from any esoteric science has been strictly consistent with modern day psychology, and the answers to stress, problem solving and money making.

Although in "The Power in Books" I recommend that you go further into Yoga breathing exercises and meditation and solitude, never forget your original material goals. The problem with esoteric knowledge is that in seeking it the Apprentice Millionaire can find himself miles away from his path toward material wealth, because although a small proportion of it *is* applicable to wealth seekers, most of it is not.

Too often I come across individuals who dabble in everything that's available, but at the same time see nothing through to its conclusion.

ADVANCE KNOWLEDGE

I once heard about a guy who regularly offered a million dollar reward to anybody who could tell him where he was going to die. When asked why he did this, he replied that if he knew for sure where he was going to die he'd never go there. Some advance knowledge is worth a lot of money.

To my mind the most valuable advance knowledge that the Apprentice Millionaire can possess is knowing that in his endeavours to succeed, he is most likely to fail just before he reaches his major objective. He may even fail many times before that, but statistics on hundreds of millionaires and successful people show that they fail just before they make the grade. Their greatest successes come after their greatest failures.

Knowing that you will possibly fail shouldn't deter you in the slightest. Neither should you try to fail; you should try to succeed, but in doing so don't be frightened of failing. There is no great success without great failure. That's advance knowledge part one. Advance knowledge part two must be indelibly printed on the mind. There is no such thing as something for nothing. A price has to be paid for each and every success.

Many times I have heard Apprentice Millionaires talk about successful motivational authors and say, "Yeah, it's all right for him to talk, all he has to do is write the books," implying that the author either hasn't or doesn't get out in the field and sell. Believe me, and I speak from experience, there is no question of anybody being able to write a motivational book without having been through the mill first. Let me qualify that. There is no question of anyone writing and getting a motivational book published which *sells well* without going through the mill first. Write a book by all means, but succeed in what you are writing about first.

PRODUCT KNOWLEDGE

A major downfall for many Apprentice Millionaires is lack of product knowledge. All too often they try to sell something that they themselves do not fully understand.

One of the greatest Eureka! experiences occurs when the subconscious mind has assimilated and organized everything at hand about the particular service or product you are trying to sell. Suddenly, Eureka! — you grasp the whole concept of what you are selling, why some people buy it and why others don't. You can clearly understand the ins and outs of the whole operation and you can see many ways of improving sales and profits.

Only when you yourself fully understand your product will you be able to sell it in a convincing manner. Read every single bit of literature available about your product. Listen to other salesmen selling your product. The way to gain product knowledge is to listen; that's why we have two ears and only one mouth.

Accept the simple fact that if you are not a millionaire or, at least, selling the amount you want, you are doing something wrong, or nothing at all.

Never, never stop trying to learn about every aspect of the product you are selling. It's no use trying to sell something over the phone by reading a sales pitch off a printed card. In order to be successful, the telephone salesman must know every aspect of the product: how much it costs, how long it takes to be delivered, how it works, what it is and why it's being sold over the phone. The whole operation has to be grasped and understood before it can be sold effectively.

Whether it is insurance, automobiles or the Amway plan you are trying to sell, you must understand it so fully yourself that you can turn it upside down and play with it like a toy if you are to market it successfully. Laziness of the mind is only an excuse for not understanding your own product.

I have always made it a point to associate with the top people in whatever field I am dealing in. Initially, I may start at the bottom, but if I can rub shoulders with those who are top salesmen in a specialist field I glean all I can from them. I watch, I listen, I learn *and I then proceed to imitate!*

Always make sure that wherever you are, whoever you are, learning the art of selling from someone with experience is the "tops." You will never learn the art of selling or product knowledge from someone who hasn't grasped the fundamentals himself. In finding top salesmen to learn from, you have to travel, you have to put yourself out, you have to work hard. When you find one, listen and learn. Most top salesmen are only too willing to impart knowledge to someone genuinely interested in learning.

PROFESSIONAL KNOWLEDGE

In my early days in business no one could ever have persuaded me that there was a professional who knew what he was doing. I dealt with them all and I never found a good one. Lawyers, bank managers, accountants, doctors were all alike — just plain painful to deal with.

A French balloonist, to his gross horror, one day found that not only had he left his compass at home, but that his balloon was rapidly losing height. He knew he had travelled a long way across the English Channel, but that's all he knew. When the balloon landed in the middle of a field an Englishman came over to see if the balloonist was all right. "Where am I?" asked the Frenchman. "You are in a balloon, in a field," said the Englishman. To which the Frenchman replied, "You must be an accountant." Yes, I am, how on earth did you know that?" said the Englishman. The Frenchman smiled and said "The information you have given me is accurate, but useless!"

Bank managers give you an umbrella and take it away when it rains. Lawyers are more intent on killing deals than making them and doctors are more interested in killing patients than curing them, or so it would appear.

With modern accounting there are dozens of ways of adding up the same sets of figures in order to come out with a dozen totally different balances. It all depends on whether you want the books to show small profit to reduce income tax liability, or large profit to enable you to borrow money more easily, or, perhaps, you want your books to reflect exactly what your business has done regardless of other considerations.

The one important point to remember when dealing with all professionals is that *you are in charge* and that your advisors are *only as good as your instructions*. You cannot expect your advisors to think for you, simply because you are the only one who knows your business. You are the one who knows the intricacies of each and every deal, the personalities behind the people you are dealing with and the *true* reasons why you are instructing a professional advisor in the first place.

It is imperative that you realize professionals only exist because of you and for your benefit, not the other way around.

Only when you grasp this knowledge will you be able to instruct the professionals to do exactly what you want and carry out your instructions. Repeat: *your* instructions.

One of the shrewdest moves you can make is to both cultivate and tame professionals whom you can understand and who understand you. It is more than probable that you will have to search these people out — but any effort directed to this cause is worthwhile.

SPECULATIVE KNOWLEDGE

Much speculation is devoted to whether inflation will keep rising, whether the economy will collapse completely, will there be a war, and what can be done?

Since the early civilizations things have always been changing. Empires fall, others rise, economies collapse and economies get built up again. Wars are lost and won.

What is needed is a success philosophy that will carry you through both good times and bad. The philosophy presented to you here is exactly what you require, for it works for the benefit of mankind regardless of whatever religious, political or economic upheavals are going on in any country in the world. It is a philosophy that works for anyone at any time, provided you use it to the letter.

In times of depression you should barter and this philosophy fits the bill ideally; all you need to know is encapsulated between the covers. Shortfalls in your knowledge of any thing or situation must be bridged by locating the knowledge you require. There are always good books available on future speculations. The doom watchers impart much knowledge that would help to make your life easier should the economy collapse or inflation get completely out of control.

During depressions, wars or political struggles there is always someone who manages to come out of it smelling like a rose. You can be that person. Don't let other people panic you. Make your own decisions. Follow the advice of your subconscious mind. Your subconscious mind is the most remarkable computer in the world for survival instincts.

BUSINESS KNOWLEDGE

It helps tremendously if one is clear in his approach to fortune building. All routes begin with the desire for money, and the route to choose is one you are happy on. People rarely succeed at anything unless they are actually having fun doing it. "Just a job," isn't going to make a fortune for you. You've got to be in a business either of your own or someone else's. If it's your own, you are going the entrepreneurial route. If it's someone else's it will usually be the corporate route, simply because you stand to make a fortune in a corporation rather than in someone else's small business (unless you go into a partnership, in which case you will be going the entrepreneurial route). This philosophy works for either route, it makes no difference. Business revolves around buying and selling, supply and demand and employees and customers. It's as easy as that.

The next choice is whether you sell a million small things with a dollar profit in each, or five-hundred large items with two-thousand dollars profit in each sale. Money is to be made either way, just as it is if you are selling ideas, services or tangible goods.

The obvious route for someone with no capital is to sell services. You can make a lot of money in labour intensive schemes, employing more and more man power as you need it. If you want to get into business and require stock and have no capital, borrow the money or talk a deal with someone. Don't let minor details like no capital put an end to your being an Apprentice Millionaire before you even start.

INTELLECTUAL KNOWLEDGE

Intellectuality is not necessarily the route to great wealth. Many of the top salesmen are of average intelligence; certainly most of the self-made millionaires are. It's fine if you are an intellectual but it's equally okay if you are not.

Wealth building requires vision, tenacity, S.S.S. and good salesmanship, not necessarily high intellect. You don't have to be brilliant to succeed in the attainment of your goals; however, you do have to keep on keeping on, and be persistent. As Bernard Baruch once said, "People of mediocre ability often achieve success because they don't know enough to quit."

The other day I heard a group of intellectuals discussing whether or not Uri Geller actually does or does not bend metal with his mind. Not once was it pointed out that Geller actually does do *something*, and that this *something* is done in front of T.V. cameras, scientists in laboratories and huge stage audiences. The intellectuals completely ignored the fact that he does this *something*, and this one thing is human accomplishment. Not once was the fact mentioned that silicon chips, computers, space rockets, laser beams, radios, television sets and telephones are all products of the human mind. In fact, they are all far greater accomplishments than bending mere spoons. When you grasp the power of the subconscious mind you, yourself, will know whether Geller actually bends metal with his mind or not.

The point being made is that all too often the intellectual is educated beyond his own intelligence and completely misses the point — a case of not being able to see the forest for the trees.

Frequently the intellectual writes above the heads of his readers and when he sells he sells above the heads of his prospects. The art of selling is not to show the customer how clever you are, but just the reverse. The customer is the "man of the moment." You must do everything within your power to make him feel great, well-liked and important. When selling, think "BIG YOU — little me." You may well be smart — but don't appear to be!

GUT KNOWLEDGE

Gut knowledge is the essence of this whole philosophy. The Eurekas! that come from the subconscious mind are what we call gut knowledge.

You will have already seen that we cannot rely on reason for sorting out our problems and generating success ideas because the simple fact is that the reasoning faculty picks up misinformation. The subconscious, however, sifts and sorts, assimilates and computes and comes up only with plans that definitely work, if put into operation by the individual who receives the plan. The subconscious mind is the key to serendipity, which is the seeming gift for making fortunate discoveries accidentally.

One must distinguish between wishful thinking and gut knowledge. Make no mistake about it, the subconscious knows your past, present and future. It can prompt you to buy a winning lottery ticket, back a horse or win a competition. Wishful thinking has a subtle habit of creeping in here and there. The Eureka! experience comes with rapidity into the mind and it's obvious that the solution or idea is right and that it's going to work. With wishful thinking, although it may be a nice thought, it's mixed with doubt and confusion.

MACHIAVELLIAN KNOWLEDGE

In the world of business there is always talk of Machiavellian methods, trickery and manipulation. Machiavelli was an advisor to the Medici in Italy during the 16th century. His knowledge of psychology was vast. He knew how to motivate and manipulate.

The secret behind his success is still used today and is just as effective now as it was then. The secret lies in talking to people in stories, metaphors, parables and fables. One of Machiavelli's favorite illustrations was to relate how Achilles was educated by Chiron, the centaur. The parable was to teach man to use both his animal and human natures. Since Chiron was semi-animal and semi-human, he was a good teacher. The Apprentice Millionaire must be like a cunning fox so that he can recognize traps, and like a ferocious lion to frighten away wolves, but he must also use his human intelligence.

Aesop used to tell his famous fables to Croesus, King of Lydia, who was reputed to be the wealthiest man in the world. Aesop discovered that this was the only way he could be heard in the king's court, and by telling fables he could say anything he liked and get away with it. By telling fables, you see, the person to whom the fable was directed could either take the hint or ignore it, but never be offended. Aesop used to take particular delight in pointing out people's faults — very subtly.

As Aesop pointed out, every man carries two wallets. He carries one in front and one behind, both full of faults. The one behind is full of his own faults and the one in front is full of his neighbours'. So it happens, said Aesop, that men are always blind to their own faults, but they never lose sight of their neighbours'.

Jesus used the parable method of teaching with such success that I doubt there is anyone living who hasn't heard his name and at least a few of the stories that relate to the happiness and success of the man.

When Machiavelli manipulated and motivated he used to do it in such a way that the maneuvers were not perceived. When you talk to employees, use motivational stories to inspire them into action. It is a common mistake to think that you can bring people around with blunt criticism. You can't, it always alienates them. Relate to people with kind and helpful stories which they can either accept or ignore as they choose. Machiavellian knowledge is telling people what they want to hear!

When you talk to people in metaphors, stories and fables you get through to their subconscious minds. They will almost always find themselves repeating the story to themselves every now and then. It might sink in so deeply that they even repeat the story to friends. It is only a matter of time before the subconscious mind directs them to carry out the story or metaphor to the letter!

GENERAL KNOWLEDGE

We have already mentioned that part of the secret of success in selling is the conversational manner and the selling of ourselves to others. General knowledge plays a great part in the conversational manner in which we conduct our sales. If you have some general knowledge it will help your conversational manner tremendously.

General knowledge can also be useful to the subconscious mind when it is computing solutions to problems and coming up with Eurekas! Don't forget that many solutions to problems come outside the frame of logical and vertical thought. Your subconscious mind may well have specialized knowledge, but to compute its Eurekas! it needs information you don't normally seek.

It is highly beneficial to go to stores and shops that you don't frequent normally. Also go to shows, musicals, museums and workshops that are not your usual scene.

Make a habit of reading daily newspapers for world events and the advertisements, to see what other people are doing. Occasionally buy a gardening or fishing magazine (or something else that is definitely not you). For the Apprentice Millionaire to suffer from tunnel vision is nothing short of a crime.

Make a point of doing things that are out of the ordinary as well as keeping in touch with the latest trends. Don't forget that although you may miss something, your subconscious may home in on something that is vitally important for the formation of its Eureka!

SELF KNOWLEDGE

In discovering the self, you will have to push yourself to the breaking point time and time again, and in doing so you will find out how resilient the human being is.

A very important fact to grasp is that when you decide to become an Apprentice Millionaire nobody will be on your side, possibly not even the people you love and those who love you. It is beyond most people's comprehension that someone who is perhaps mediocre, or who has never achieved much, is *definitely* going to be a millionaire in x, y or z number of years.

Never let this negation overwhelm you, not even if it comes from your closest friends or loved ones. This negation is something every millionaire or successful person has had to put up with and ignore. It's nice if you get positive support, but don't expect it. At times it will appear that you have taken on the world single handedly; you probably will have done, and if you keep on keeping on, you will win!

Make a point of keeping self knowledge what it is. It is exactly what it says it is: all the knowledge of yourself, the things you can do and can't do, and the things you want to achieve. The things you have failed at and the reason why.

All your self knowledge is what is going to convert you into a millionaire and a success. It is very acceptable to get help from other people. Other people's skills in various fields may very well exceed your own, but ultimately your success is going to depend on your self knowledge. I have never come across anybody who has made a success or a million dollars for anybody else. It is up to you to achieve your goals. Self knowledge is one of the tools that will help you.

ACQUISITION OF KNOWLEDGE

The Apprentice Millionaire can adopt a certain air of superiority, simply because he has one thing at his fingertips: he knows where to acquire knowledge on a day-to-day basis which relates to his life, his business, or any other area in which he is interested.

The only people without problems are those in cemeteries. Start your acquisition of knowledge by acquiring every bit of known data pertaining to your problems. Start by going to the local library and feeding your subconscious enough material to enable it to compute a solution to your problem. It doesn't matter what your problem is, there is a wealth of information about it. Millions of people before you have had problems with stress, depression, debt, impotence, shyness, worry, insomnia, loss of a loved one, disability, headaches — you name it — someone has written about it.

Write for advice to magazines and newspapers which specialize in your area of concern. Determine to solve the problems by acquiring sufficient knowledge.

Do not forget that many mail-order book companies carry books which specifically discuss the types of problems we have been discussing.

Take the guesswork out of it, ask around, talk to people, ask for advice. Libraries, museums, colleges, extra study courses, weekend seminars, and university bookstores are just a few of the sources available to you. If necessary seek professional advice; thumb through the Yellow Pages. Help is available.

It is very important to grasp the fact that problems have solutions. It is even more important to remember that the knowledge you acquire may not give you the answer to your problem directly, but it is grist for the subconscious mill, which will compute your solution for you.

ZOOM SECRETS!

1. Practice learning how to stop the internal dialogue. There are many ways of doing this — using a mantra, or staring blankly at a pile of leaves or a bunch of flowers. Walking on your own in the country is another good way. Keep your unfocused eyes on the horizon, but try not to totally lose your peripheral vision.

2. Don't get too involved in the esoteric sciences. Total absorption in them may lead you away from your original goals.

3. Don't be frightened of failing. Never forget there is no such thing as something for nothing.

4. Study and learn every conceivable aspect of the product or service you sell. Cultivate your product knowledge to the point you understand it so well that you can "play" with it.

5. Professionals exist merely for your benefit. *You* must instruct *them*. When you deal with the professionals YOU ARE IN CHARGE.

6. During economic depressions never let people panic you. Follow the advice of your subconscious mind.

7. Decide whether you are going to go the entrepreneurial route or the corporate route. Also decide whether you are going to sell millions of small things with a small margin in each or a few large items with a large margin.

8. It doesn't matter how smart you are, never show it to a prospect. Think "BIG YOU — little me."

9. When a Eureka! presents itself it is obvious that the solution will work or that the idea is right. Wishful thinking can be distinguished from Eurekas! because it is mixed with doubt and confusion.

10. Machiavellian knowledge is telling people what they want to hear. Tell fables, metaphors and stories; the message will sink in subconsciously.

11. Go to new stores, different shops, and shows you wouldn't normally see. Read books and magazines that are not your scene. Increase your general knowledge. Give the subconscious mind something to work with.
12. Grasp the fact that problems have solutions. Read and study as much as you can pertaining to any problem. Then give the subconscious mind time to compute a solution for you.

CHAPTER 14

THE POWER AND THE GLORY

"If thou canst believe, all things
are possible to him that believeth."

MARK 9:23

As an ultra-ambitious entrepreneur I used to rotate at
at such a rate of knots I nearly self-destructed. There
had to be another way of carrying on and achieving.
The solution I found was meditation in S.S.S. and the
study of much psychology, most of which I have covered in detail.

I have already mentioned that Jung was my favourite psychologist and his works led me down many path-
ways. Looking back on his years of work and research
Jung realized that he had never been able to cure any
patient of any serious psychological disorder unless he
had been able to induce in that patient a "religious
attitude" toward life. Furthermore, the patient had to
adopt that attitude willingly rather than have it forced
upon him.

On the strength of this I decided to do some research of my own. As usual I began by taking the whole
thing down to its nuts and bolts; treading where angels
fear to tread, so to speak. By the time I had finished, I
realized I had found the ultimate power. What is presented to you here is the apex of my philosophy.

The two words that appear over and over again in the bible are "faith" and "belief." The main theme of the bible is faith and belief. In the New Testament alone, those two words crop up over five hundred times. Belief is very powerful, very much misunderstood and very difficult to explain — convincingly. For thousands of years apostles, preachers, ministers and sages have been preaching the gospels and telling people to "Have faith" or "You must believe." On and on, ranting and raving. But no matter how enthusiastically or emphatically the minister smashes his clenched fist into the palm of his other hand, no matter how loud he shouts, rants or raves, unless he explains what belief or faith is, all is lost.

There are two types of belief — one is spiritual belief, the other is psychological belief. They are very different, both very powerful and can be used individually or together. The best analogy is to take a car with a conventional shift gear. There are two ways to increase the engine power. One is to push on the gas pedal, increasing the supply of fuel to the cylinders. The other way is to change gear. If you wanted to use them together you could change into a lower gear and depress the gas pedal and you'd be off like the proverbial rocket!

So it is with the two types of belief. You either use them on their own, or together. Psychologists have proved that human capabilities are increased to almost supernatural proportions when psychological belief is exercised. Religious leaders have proved that "All things are possible with spiritual belief." Use the two beliefs together and you'll be invincible!

PSYCHOLOGICAL BELIEF

A young mother of five children was worn out before the day had even begun. She still had all the dishes to wash, beds to make, the dinner to cook, the children to clean up after and the baby's diapers to change. There she was, feeling terrible, when she suddenly remembered a pep pill her friend had given to her the day before and which she had slipped into her apron pocket. She popped it into her mouth and before long was merrily working away, cleaning, polishing and cooking. Life was a labour of love, she felt good to be alive. Sometime later she took off her apron and in doing so the pep pill that her friend had given her fell out of the apron pocket and onto the floor. What she had popped into her mouth was one of her children's sweets! What caused the amazing transformation was psychological belief.

An old lady suffered terribly with arthritis. She tried every remedy she knew and went to every doctor and specialist she could find. One day she bumped into a friend of hers who suggested she wear a copper bracelet around her wrist. The friend told her that she, too, had tried every cure imaginable with no success until she tried the copper bracelet. The old lady did try it, and found 100 percent success! Again psychological belief worked wonders. Medical science cannot find any reason why copper should cure arthritis, but any psychologist worth his salt will tell you a plastic bracelet will work just as well, providing it is used with belief!

A young boy went down to his doctor's office because he had some warts on the back of his hand. To his surprise the doctor paid him five cents for each wart with the assurance that now that he had bought and paid for them they would disapppear. Of course the warts disappeared. The boy believed they would. He believed that since the doctor had paid for the warts they were now the doctor's and would disappear. And they did.

Every day in every doctor's office across the country prescriptions are written out for tens of thousands of placebos. Patients swallow these little sugar coated pills. The majority of them get cured of whatever ailment it was that bothered them. Generally, the placebo is an innocuous milk-sugar tablet dressed up like an authentic pill. Even the colour and taste have something to do with the amount of belief the pill creates. Slightly bitter, and pastel green or red, seem to work the best! "Placebo" means "I shall please" and, with the aid of psychological belief, they normally do!

In parts of Africa where black magic is still practiced, belief plays a large role. The witch doctor has to be seen or heard by either the victim or the victim's friends (so they can tell the victim) before the witch doctor can "cast the spell or place the hex." This is done in a number of ways, but the important issue is that before any black magic can take place the victim must believe he is the victim of the spell. It would be absolutely futile if the witch doctor were to point the bone without telling or showing anyone.

A friend of mine was very shy and reserved — a real introvert — but he longed for a relationship with a mutual friend of ours, Molly. I realized he was just too embarrassed to try to date her, so one day I said to him, "I was talking to Molly yesterday and she really likes you, but she's too shy to take the initiative. If you ask her for a date she will say yes." He believed what I told him, and he dated Molly the same evening. If he had not believed that I had spoken to Molly, he would not have approached her.

Some time ago, in my office, we decided to play a stupid joke on an associate, not realizing how far it could go. We all agreed, unbeknownst to Guy, that we would each periodically tell him how ill he looked. When he was first told he simply laughed and carried on working. Next time around he admitted he felt a bit queasy, and by mid-afternoon when just about everybody in the office had said how terrible he looked, Guy actually ran to the bathroom and vomited! He had finally succumbed to our repeated suggestion. He *believed* he was ill, and therefore he actually became ill.

Now we have enough examples with which to do some analysis. Two seeming paradoxes become apparent. The first one is that there can be no psychological belief without using a big white lie. Secondly, the only way you can produce a big white lie is to use it on someone else, or on yourself *accidentally*, as in the case of the woman taking her child's sweet. You can't *intentionally* use this type of psychological belief on yourself because you would be aware of the big white lie. When a doctor prescribes a placebo to cure his patient's ailment it is the psychological belief that cures him. The big white lie is that the patient believes he's getting medicine and, to fulfill the second half of the belief formula, the doctor uses it on the patient. It would be futile for the doctor to prescribe placebos for himself, simply because he would be aware of the big white lie.

Now we can see there are two types of psychological belief. One, the type of belief you use on other people, and the other, the type you use on yourself.

USING PSYCHOLOGICAL BELIEF ON OTHER PEOPLE

When I'm selling, I keep up my belief in the product all the time. I show my belief in myself by my enthusiasm and my excitement. Many an Apprentice Millionaire fails to make sales for the simple reason that although he starts out with belief and shows it through his enthusiasm, when his prospect fails to alter his facial expression, show enthusiasm or interest in the presentation the salesman then loses his belief and the prospect knows it. You *have* to believe in yourself before others will believe in you.

Psychological belief is so powerful that you must keep up your enthusiasm and belief in yourself during the entire time you are facing your prospect, no matter what he says, no matter what he does, no matter what his facial expression. And, you must give time for the psychological belief to have its effect on the prospect.

Remember Guy in the earlier story? We kept hammering away, telling him he looked ill, until he believed it. You must keep on and on at your prospect in a conversational manner that is full of enthusiasm and belief. Let that belief envelop him; it can't fail!

Even when your prospect appears not to have the slightest bit of interest, keep up your belief in yourself and your product. He might come back later when the belief has had time to soak in and get hold of him, and he might say "I've been thinking about what you were saying, and you've really sold me on the idea — let me have a dozen!"

It is essential to remember that whatever you put over to a prospect in the form of a big white lie will be believed providing you do not let on that it is a big white lie.

When I was training a specialty salesman to sell a particular product, I explained to him that the next customer I sent him to would definitely buy the goods because the sale was pre-arranged. I also warned the salesman that the prospect was a funny eccentric individual who would put the salesman through hell before he would actually place the order. I told him to remember everything I had taught him: sell in a conversational manner, establish subconscious rapport, sell to the three systems, gather information in order to sell, enthuse over the customer's house as well as over the product and keep the strongest sales pitch until the last moment. "But whatever you do," I told him, "come away with the order." Of course it was just as I told him. He found the man full of resistance and very uncooperative. But the trainee salesman still kept hammering away because he believed that the sale was prearranged. He came away with the order! Make sure you understand that without the big white lie there is no psychological belief!

Another illustration: in the course of fighting off creditors I learned many loopholes and ways around the debt problem. I had the Eureka! that I ought to set up a consultancy business.

When the advertisements came out, I was flooded with business and had more clients than I could handle. Now do you imagine that if I had told those clients that I had debt problems of my own, they would have acted on anything I told them? No. Instead I used the big white lie — that I was a business consultant of many years' standing and knew how to fight creditors, reduce overheads and increase business. In fact, I didn't even tell my clients anything at all about what I was or what I wasn't. I let them assume I was a consultant of many years' standing, and they could *tell* I was because of my confidence, enthusiasm and belief. You can't get others to believe in you until you believe in yourself. I acted as if I was an experienced consultant, and I believed I was!

You have had dramatic illustrations of how to use psychological belief on other people. When we use psychological belief on ourselves we have to use a completely different method. Should you prescribe yourself placebos they would be valueless because to you there is no big white lie. When you use psychological belief on other people you are presenting something to their conscious minds and, like the ego, explained in a previous chapter, it accepts what is put in front of it.

USING PSYCHOLOGICAL BELIEF ON YOURSELF

When you use psychological belief on yourself, you have to use a completely different method. When you know you are telling yourself a big white lie, the knowledge creates instant disbelief.

When you use psychological belief on yourself, the only way you can make the belief work is to tap, tap, tap the belief onto your subconscious mind over a period of time. When you visualize your desires, believe you have already acquired the goal you are seeing. All we do is follow the preceding chapters on goals and mind power. We visualize our desires, our wants, our goals.

The subconscious mind has more than enough power to overcome the disbelief created by your knowing that you are not really a millionaire, provided that you tap, tap, tap the big white lie onto your subconscious mind every night and every morning. Seeing with the mind's eye is believing! When we tap, tap, tap the big white lie (that we are millionaires or we own a Rolls Royce or a pink Cadillac) onto our subconscious minds, the subconscious mind eventually takes over and makes the big white lie a tangible reality by producing a Eureka! which will be a foolproof plan or idea for the attainment of the big white lie.

Visualize your goals in your mind's eye. Do the same kinesthetically and auditorily. See your car in every detail, its leather interior, its magnesium wheels and its glossy paintwork. Feel the cold air from the air conditioning, feel the tightness of the precision steering, feel the low center of gravity. Hear the purr of the engine, hear the squeal of the radials and hear the electric windows roll up. Become overjoyed that you own it and drive it. Jump up and down with the sheer exuberance that comes from knowing you are a millionaire. Go into raptures when you see your goals in your mind's eye. The more joy, excitement and emotion you put into your visualizing, the sooner the subconscious mind will produce its Eureka! Emotion counts as much as anything when you're visualizing your goals. The emotions of seeing, feeling, and hearing create the belief!

The subconscious mind is powerful enough to take over and provide Eurekas! so long as you program it properly. The belief is *created* by seeing your goals in your mind's eye, feeling with emotion and telling yourself you have achieved them. In other words, even if you can't believe consciously that you are a millionaire or own a Rolls Royce, as long as you visualize as described, that visualizing alone will tap, tap, tap the belief onto the subconscious mind.

Belief is absolutely essential for this philosophy to work; therefore, it is imperative you realize that there is no other known way of using psychological belief on oneself other than *repeated affirmation of your goals and desires to the subconscious mind* through the practice of visualization. Visualizing is believing without belief, beyond belief!

SPIRITUAL BELIEF

To clarify the meaning of spiritual belief, we will use the definition of religion put forth by Paul Tillich, the German theologian. He called religion a system that deals with ultimate concerns.

The best example of spiritual belief is that of Jesus bringing Lazarus back from the dead. There would have been no big white lie because Lazarus was dead anyway, he couldn't have known what was going on. What brought him back to life was spiritual belief.

They say that what the fool doesn't understand, he laughs at, but no Apprentice Millionaire can afford not to take advantage of every conceivable power that is available. Just because we don't understand things fully doesn't mean they don't work. Vast amounts of evidence are stacking up all the time about miracles, prayer and spiritual belief. I think it necessary that I make my own case quite clear. I believe in the subconscious mind. I believe in the cubic centimeter of chance. And I believe in God.

For all my worldly desires I rely on my subconscious mind. From time to time the cubic centimetre of chance appears, and I may or may not recognize it. I usually do, but not always. When I am really troubled, or have a desperate problem that needs a solution and I don't think my subconscious has time to assimilate the problem or I require a miracle to happen, I pray to God.

Spiritual belief works on both oneself and others. Distance makes no difference on the effectiveness of prayer. You can work spiritual belief on others and they don't even have to be conscious of it. There are literally thousands of books packed with evidence of healings, miracles and the power of prayer. It is up to the individual to reach out and choose his own spiritual belief. It is not the purpose of this book, nor my intention, to force it on anyone. However, in the writing of this book on how to obtain power, it automatically becomes my duty to point out this phenomenal power available to you for the taking. Many millionaires have been quick to realize this power. It works for the benefit of all mankind, and all you have to do is believe!

Some time ago a number of theologians got together with some very learned judges, lawyers and legal brains to see if they could find any untruths in the bible. Using the same methods they would for a court case the lawyers cross referenced every ounce of information available from the bible with modern knowledge of the Holy Land supplied by historians and cartographers. There was unanimous agreement among everyone involved that because all the details tallied so perfectly, what was written in the great book could be accepted as the truth.

So powerful is spiritual belief that many people have found great relief from their anxieties and sufferings by writing their problems down on a sheet of paper and carefully putting it in the bible. Others slept with their bibles under their pillows and in doing so found tremendous comfort, relief from stress and belief that they were delivered from evil.

I have already pointed out to you that the way to get through to other people's subconscious minds is to speak in parables, stories and metaphors. Jesus used the parable method in his teachings and indeed the whole bible can be thought of as a metaphor.

Explaining to a salesman that some of the seed he sows will land on the rocks, some will be suffocated by thorns and the rest of it will grow, brings more results than telling him he can't expect to make a sale at every door he knocks on.

Every day in business you must do a few of the things you don't like doing in order to reap a harvest. And don't forget — as you sow, so shall you reap. One could go on indefinitely with examples, but the idea behind this book is to show you a principle, not a specific way. The principle, in this instance, is that in speaking in parables and metaphors you get through to the subconscious mind.

To clear up a few well-known quotes from the bible, I want to pick them out and highlight them, and then add a few comments in hopes of enhancing and clarifying them. The following are some key interpretations of key quotes.

"BECOME AS LITTLE CHILDREN."

Children are usually happy smiling creatures, always up to something and having fun. If a child does get upset it is usually for only a very short while; soon he is back to his normal self again. (I would like to qualify this by saying that children who are not happy, and there are many, are generally the product of someone else's unhappiness, a broken home, or abuse. Normally children are happy if they are brought up in a happy, loving environment.)

Children have a terrific acceptance of things, ideas, circumstances and change. Should you make some outrageous statement to little children they will accept it without question. You might say, "Tomorrow we're going to see Santa Claus, some fairies and some trolls," and it's accepted, no questions asked. Also, little children have no difficulty seeing themselves as anything they wish to be. One little child will become a spaceman simply by putting a cardboard box over his head. Another will become a soldier by slinging a piece of wood on his shoulder, like a gun. A third will become an airplane just by putting his arms out and screaming like a jet. Why should we wish to become as little children, and even if we wanted to, how do we go about it?

To take the first part of the question, we must become as little children to lead happier lives. We must become as little children and accept great ideas and plans although they might be outlandish. To make that million, you are going to have to do something pretty outlandish or dynamic. Accept that fact, the same as a little child would, without question. Undoubtedly millionaires and successful people believe in their ideas with an almost childlike belief. It was Ernest Holmes who wrote, "Faith is a mental attitude which is so convinced of its own idea — which so completely accepts it — that any contradiction is unthinkable and impossible."

The reason why little children are so happy and accepting is because they don't have the incessant internal dialogue that adults do. Admittedly they have it to some small degree, but not to the extent of an adult. Adults have a mind-tape loop playing repeatedly, every minute of the day, of all the failures, traumas, heartbreaks, and reasons why things can't be done. To become as a little child, stop the internal dialogue and you have arrived!

"IF YE HAVE FAITH AS A GRAIN OF MUSTARD SEED, YE SHALL SAY UNTO THIS MOUNTAIN, REMOVE HENCE TO YONDER PLACE: AND IT SHALL REMOVE: AND NOTHING SHALL BE IMPOSSIBLE UNTO YOU."

The statement above probably causes more disbelief and amazement than any other quote from the bible. We have seen faith and belief work to extraordinary degrees. You must have faith in yourself, your business and in others;

it is the ultimate power. There is nothing strange about faith the size of a mustard seed making mountains move; accept it fully.

The brilliant physicist, David Bohm, computed the "zero-point energy" due to quantum-mechanical fluctuations in a single cubic centimetre of space, and arrived at the energy of 10^{38} ergs. A single cubic centimetre is approximately the size of a grain of mustard, and yet Bohm translates his ergs into the equivalent of about 10 billion tons of uranium. Admittedly a lot has to be done before the formula works, but in the same manner as mechanical, thermal, chemical, electrical, luminous and gravitational energies have been discovered and harnessed it's only a matter of time before Bohm's formula becomes reality. It's the same way that Einstein's $E = mc^2$ turned into the atomic bomb in a relatively short space of time. Pick a few mustard seeds for yourself and keep them in your pocket as a constant reminder of the small amount of faith you need to achieve great heights. Remind yourself also that when none other than the steel billionaire, Andrew Carnegie, was asked the secret of his phenomenal success he replied, "Faith in myself, faith in others and faith in my business."

"BE CAREFUL FOR NOTHING."

All too often does the Appentice Millionaire barter his chance of success for security. No one who has ever made the grade has been able to do this. The man who succeeds is "careful for nothing," he is prepared to put everything on the line in order to win!

By now you should have more than just an understanding of the principles of success. The Apprentice Millionaire will follow his subconscious mind even if it is in *opposition to all* those around him.

MONEY IS THE ROOT OF ALL EVIL.

Since this must be the most ubiquitous misquote of all time, I have not placed quotation marks around it.

Nowhere in the bible does it say, "Money is the root of all evil." What it does say is, "The love of money is the root of all evil," something totally different.

The love of money refers to the emotion of greed. When someone says, "Money is the root of all evil," he is talking about tangible money. He is saying that the money it takes to build churches, hospitals and schools is evil, which of course is absurd.

A less popular quote from the bible is: "A feast is made for laughter, and wine maketh merry: but money answereth all things." And the truest statement of all was made by George Bernard Shaw, when he said "The lack of money is the root of all evil."

"WHAT THINGS SO EVER YE DESIRE, WHEN YE PRAY, BELIEVE THAT YE RECEIVE THEM, AND YE SHALL HAVE THEM."

If we analyse the foregoing, the most powerful statement in the world, it simply means:

Whatever you desire: That is your list of goals; as previously discussed, it can be made up of both material and intangible desires.

When you pray: That is your repeated affirmation to the subconscious mind, God, or both; the asking. Use both psychological belief and spiritual belief together and you'll be invincible!

Believe that you receive them: We have already discussed in great detail the seeing of things in the mind's eye, the visualizing of things already received; the pink Cadillac, country mansion, bank account with a million dollars in it. You see in your mind's eye that you are already in possession of the things you desire. Re-read "The Secret of Goals."

And You shall receive them: There has never been a case, ever, of anyone following the foregoing statement who has not received what he prayed for and visualized, provided he prayed and visualized every night and every morning and believed that he had already received what he was praying for.

"ASK AND YE SHALL RECEIVE."

Ask and Ye Shall Receive can be interpreted as *Talk and Grow Rich*. This is further backed up with two more quotes, "What you say is what you get" and "Death and life are in the power of the tongue." For further proof about "Ask and ye shall receive," re-read the chapters "Dynamic Psychology," "The Orator Is King" and "Talk and Grow Rich." The bible makes a great issue of asking and talking. "In the beginning was the word . . . " To me that is significant in itself and this whole philosophy is molded around talking. The word is the important thing. The word of Moses divided the Red Sea, the word of Elias changed the waters so that they were strong enough to carry iron across the surface. Any success you are likely to have, *and you will*, is going to come directly or indirectly as a result of your talking to someone!

"FOR LACK OF VISION MY PEOPLE PERISH."

There is no future for the person who does not visualize his goals or future simply because everything that is done or made has to come in the form of visualized thought first. We have discussed at great length in "The Secret of Goals" and "Mind Power" seeing in your mind's eye the repetition of mental images and visualizing your desires in your scrapbook. By visualizing your desires regularly you are automatically taking advantage of the most powerful words in the world: belief and faith. There can be no belief or faith if you do not visualize your goals. It is the ONLY way to develop the emotions of belief and faith for your own use.

"I WILL LIFT UP MINE EYES UNTO THE HILLS WHENCE COMETH MY HELP."

The principle of power, that is, S.S.S. (Silence, Stillness and Solitude) comes to everybody's aid. We have studied the principle of power in great depth. The solutions to problems and new ideas are generated in S.S.S. The best place to achieve S.S.S. is undoubtedly up in the hills but this is not always practicable, especially for city dwellers. To achieve S.S.S. in the big city, churches fill the bill admirably. Churches are usually very quiet and you can sit in the back pew for hours every day in S.S.S. and nobody will disturb you. Libraries run a second best. But neither place beats the hills or the desert. Every great religious leader used the power of S.S.S. by spending long periods of time in the hills or desert: Moses, Jesus, Gandhi, Buddha, Confucius and Mohammed, to mention a few.

"GOD IS LIGHT."

Gurus of the Eastern world are so far advanced with their mind-power techniques that top universities of the Western world are beginning to study them. They are so far advanced that they prevent mental disorder before it even happens, believing that prevention is better than cure. "Guru" means, literally, "one who dispels darkness." Modern psychologists and psychiatrists dispel darkness in others but unfortunately in doing so take the whole weight of the world on their shoulders and destroy their own minds. Alcoholism among psychiatrists is rife and they have the highest of all suicide rates. The solution to the problem can be found in turning to God. God is Light. God dispels darkness.

"FAITH WITHOUT WORKS IS DEAD."

No matter what philosophy you study, follow or use, faith without works is dead. In the chapter "Action Is Power," we only scratch the surface of what must be done in order for us to achieve. We must act on the Eurekas! that come from the subconscious mind. We must grab that cubic centimeter of chance when it presents itself. Action is one of the main ingredients of success. Re-read "Action Is Power" until it is not only part of you, but until it is you!

To be of any financial benefit whatsoever this philosophy must be read, not once but many times, until the subconscious mind takes over and you don't want to stop reading it. I close with the words of perhaps one of the greatest orators the world has ever known, Winston Churchill: "Now this is not the end. It is not even the beginning of the end. But it is, perhaps, the end of the beginning."

You'd better believe it!

ZOOM SECRETS!

1. There can be no psychological belief without a big white lie. When you are selling you have to put over that big white lie with confidence and enthusiasm, as though it were really true, to enable the belief to work. You have to believe in yourself, before others will believe in you.

2. To use psychological belief on yourself you must, because you know about the big white lie, tap, tap, tap, the subconscious mind over a period of time. You do this by visualizing your goals as though they have already materialized.

3. Spiritual belief can be used for yourself and others. Pray to God for anything you desire. Believe that what you pray for has already materialized.

4. Talk in parables and metaphors and get deep into people's subconscious minds.

5. Use spiritual belief and psychological belief together and you'll be invincible!

AFTERWARNING

Since time immemorial warnings have been issued against using power for evil and negative purposes. Nearly five hundred years before Christ, Confucius, the great Chinese sage, taught the character "Shu." Jesus taught the Western world exactly the same thing: "Whatsoever ye would that men should do unto you, do even so unto them for this is the law of the prophets." Certain sects or communities would say, "If you live by the sword you shall die by the sword." The law of Karma teaches us the same thing, that if we are evil we get paid in evil.

All of these philosophies revolve around one thing: the human mind. Man is not born with a conscience. It develops as he grows. This is the sole reason why "What you do not like done to you, do not do to others" works. Because, whether you like it or not, if you use the material in this book for evil and negative purposes, the power of your own mind, your own conscience and the subconscious minds of others, will cause your efforts to boomerang and destroy you. I cannot tell you anything more emphatically.

Because of the very nature of the way in which the subconscious mind works, beware of zooming in on other people's ideas. Many of the people you talk to have a superabundance of ideas. Many of these ideas come from their subconscious minds. On many an occasion someone has grasped a brilliant idea from the subconscious of someone else, put it into operation and failed. The reason they fail is simple. The subconscious mind created the idea around all that particular person's experience, assets, liabilities and mental images. If that person had put the idea into operation he would have been bound to succeed. Now I am not saying that other people's ideas are always to be dismissed. What I am saying is beware, for although you may receive the idea, you may not receive all the hundreds of thousands of components that went into its conception. Those components may be of vital importance for bringing the idea to fruition and successful conclusion. Because the subconscious mind plots and plans around the individual's assets, liabilities, knowledge and experience, you may, even though you receive the idea, not have the background sufficient to carry it out. For the very same reason, have no fear about anybody trying to imitate your business, ideas and plans. Adopt the attitude outlined in Rudyard Kipling's "The Mary Gloster." "They copied all they could follow, but they couldn't copy my mind, / And I left them sweating and stealing a year and a half behind."

Never before have such accurate and explicit instructions for the accumulation of wealth been committed to writing. Never before have such workable and manipulative psychological tools been divulged. Without a doubt the world's most powerful book is in your possession. Nevertheless, we still have the human factor, namely "you" to contend with. If anyone were to ask me what the chances were of "you" succeeding in your endeavours, I would want to ask a few questions before I replied.

Have you made the unwavering decision to be rich? Have you committed all your goals to writing, in the present tense? Have you got a scrapbook full of pictures of all the things you desire? Do you visualize these goals every night and every morning with belief and emotion? Do you take regular time out to listen to your subconscious mind? Do you follow through with action on the things your subconscious mind tells you to do — to the letter? Do you establish subconscious rapport with your prospects *before* you try to sell them? Do you sell to *their* representational system?

If you answer an emphatic "YES!" to these questions, you will succeed — psychological law will see to that! If your answer is a halfhearted "no," then read the book again, only this time put each suggestion into practice as you go along. Having done that, when you arrive at this page once again you too will be able to answer an emphatic "YES!" and you, too, will succeed!

Write now, for details of The Apprentice Millionaires Club, further books and a fabulous business opportunity:

Apprentice Millionaires Club
70 Tilehurst Road
London SW18 3ET
England

Apprentice Millionaires Club
P.O. Box 218
West Court
Cairns 4870
Australia

BIBLIOGRAPHY

Altshuler and Comalli, in the *Journal of Auditory Research*, Washington, D.C.

Bach-y-Rita, P. *Brain Mechanisms in Sensory Substitution*. New York: Academic Press, 1972.

Bandler, R., and Grinder, J. *Patterns of the Hypnotic Techniques of Milton H. Erickson, M.D.* Cupertino, Calif.: Meta Publications, 1975.

Bandler, R., and Grinder, J. *The Structure of Magic I*. Palo Alto: Science and Behavior Books, 1975.

Bandler, R., and Grinder, J. *The Structure of Magic II*. Science and Behavior Books, 1976.

Bandler, R., and Grinder, J. *Frogs into Princes*. Real People Press, 1979.

Bateson, G. *Steps to an Ecology of Mind*. New York: Ballantine Books, 1972.

Castaneda, Carlos. *The Teachings of Don Juan*. Pocket Books.

Castaneda, Carlos. *A Separate Reality*. Pocket Books.

Castaneda, Carlos. *Journey to Ixtlan*. Pocket Books.

Castaneda, Carlos. *Tales of Power*. Pocket Books.

Chomsky, N. *Aspects of the Theory of Syntax*. Cambridge, Mass.: MIT Press, 1965.

Chomsky, N. *Syntactic Structures*. The Hague: Mouton, 1957.

Dimond, S., and Beaumont, K. *Hemispheric Functions in the Human Brain*. New York: John Wiley & Sons, 1974.

Fagen, J. (ed.). *Gestalt Therapy Now*. Palo Alto: Science and Behavior Books, 1970.

Gazzaniga, M. *The Bisected Brain*. New York: Appleton, Century, & Croft, 1974.

Haley, J. (ed.). *Advanced Techniques of Hypnosis and Therapy: Selected Papers of Milton H. Erickson, M.D.* New York: Grune and Stratton, 1967.

Haley, J. *Strategies of Psychotherapy*. New York: Grune and Stratton, 1963.

Hill, Napoleon. *Think and Grow Rich*. Fawcett, 1978.

Jackson, D.D. *Therapy, Communication and Change*. Palo Alto: Science and Behavior Books, 1968.

Laing, R.D. *The Politics of the Family and Other Essays*. London: Vintage Books, 1972.

Pearce, Joseph Chilton. *The Crack in the Cosmic Egg*. Pocket Books

Pearce, Joseph Chilton. *Exploring the Crack in the Cosmic Egg*. Pocket Books

Perls, F. *The Gestalt Approach: Eyewitness to Therapy*. Palo Alto: Science and Behavior Books, 1973.

Russell, B. *Principia Mathematica*. London: Cambridge University Press, 1910.

Satir, V. *Conjoint Family Therapy*. Palo Alto: Science and Behavior Books, 1964.

Satir, V. *Helping Families to Change*. Hays, Kansas: The High Plains Comprehensive Community Mental Health Center, 1972.

Satir, V. *Peoplemaking*. Palo Alto: Science and Behavior Books, 1972.

Schuchman, G., and Burgi, E.J., in the *Journal of Auditory Research*, Washington, D.C.

Watzlawick, P.; Weakland, J.; and Fisch, R. *Change*. New York: W. Norton, 1974.